Fields of God

Fields of God

Mark Roques

Authentic
LIFESTYLE

Copyright © 2003 Mark Roques

First published in 2003 by Authentic Lifestyle

09 08 07 06 05 04 03   7 6 5 4 3 2 1

Authentic Lifestyle is an imprint of Authentic Lifestyle,
PO Box 300, Carlisle, Cumbria CA3 0QS, UK
Box 1047, Waynesboro, GA 30830-2047, USA
www.paternoster-publishing.com

British Library Cataloguing in Publication Data

A catalogue record for this book is available from the British
Library

ISBN 1-85078-506-6

Cover design by Jon Birch
Printed in Great Britain by
Cox and Wyman Ltd., Cardiff Road, Reading

To Paul Chaplin and David Tickner
In hope and with love

Contents

Acknowledgements

There are so many people I would like to thank who have helped me in crafting this book about the beautiful game. I can only mention a few of them. Without doubt Ron Atkinson's poetical outpourings are a dream come true. Thank you Big Ron. I would also like to praise Hugh Grear for his cheeky, witty suggestions, Jimmy Tottle for his encouragement and constructive comment and Mark Cripps for his imaginative cartoons. Jon Birch, that endearing Arsenal fan has supported me in countless ways and I thank him for his cover. Richard Russell has helped many of us to understand the biblical story and I am continually surprised by his vast and wonderful knowledge. I must also thank Albert Wolters and Calvin Seerveld for their inspired teaching. My wife, Anne, has shaped my thinking about the teaching of Jesus and I owe her an enormous debt. Lastly I thank my dear friend Mr James Dean Tickner for his infectious charm, warmth and *joie de vivre*. Your knowledge about the game is a source of enduring comfort and consolation in these twilight years of middle age.

Introduction

Recently I went into a Christian bookshop and asked the woman working there if there were any books on the kingdom of God. She looked at me rather warily and stuttered the kingdom of what? She proceeded to ransack her shop and eventually came up with an obscure and scholarly book of some five hundred pages. Close inspection of the tome revealed arcane Hebrew, Greek and German footnotes and numerous technical terms such as *eschatological*, *parousia*, *Nah-erwartung* and *basileia*. I was also disappointed to find no references to *little eyebrows*, *killer passes*, *nutmegs* and *playing in instalments*.[1]

'Is this the only book you have?' I probed. The woman was most emphatic. This was the only one. 'So you don't have anything on football and the kingdom of God, then?'

The woman was becoming slightly impatient and her cheerful demeanour was ebbing away. In the bitterness of failure she roused herself to one final stab at success. 'Do you mean a book about heaven and going to heaven – because we have hundreds like that?'

---

[1] For those who are unacquainted with technical football terms we suggest that you peruse the glossary on page 130.

Sullenly I turned away and left the shop.

Whenever I tell people that I am writing a book about football and the kingdom of God, I seem to elicit chuckles, titters and general merriment. Somehow the two don't seem to go together. For some the kingdom of God concerns *souls* and *going to heaven*. For others the kingdom of God refers to church and churchy activities. There are those who equate the kingdom of God with a fair and humane political system. On all these views football has little if nothing to do with *religion*. There are also people who are genuinely puzzled by the expression the *kingdom of God*. They are surprised to learn that Jesus frequently mentioned the topic. We must be candid and frank. There is widespread confusion and ignorance as to what Jesus meant when he spoke about the kingdom of God. This book will introduce its readers to this crunch concept by exploring the colourful and entertaining world of football.

But before we go any further I need to introduce you to one of my best mates. His name is Jim Tickner and just like me, Jim is a football nut. He loves the game and can often be heard discussing the finer points of *drag-backs*, *reducers* and *step-overs*. Jim is a passionate supporter of Bristol Rovers and he lives forty yards from their ground in North Bristol. Jim is no stranger to the trials and tribulations that football can bestow upon its devotees and tragically his beloved team do not always respond to his deepest cravings. Sitting in Jim's living room on Wednesday evenings our mutual passions erupt as we talk football and God ... almost in the same breath. This book is the fruit of our many conversations about the beautiful game and the God who created the game at the very dawn of time.

The beautiful game and the ugly game

Let us try to imagine a fantastic world with perfect football clubs and leagues. All the players love each other and the football is a delight to behold. Deft flicks, elusive dribbling and outrageous scissor kicks are the order of the day. Brazilian ball skills flourish abundantly. Cheeky, friendly banter infuses the very warp and woof of the game. Certainly there is drive and competition as teams struggle to win the FA Cup but there is always fair play, honesty and good humour. Players might clumsily lunge and foul their opponents but good grace abounds. When Derek scores with his blistering thirty-yard piledriver, everyone applauds and claps. When Berty caresses the ball around the park and delivers the killer pass, there are shouts of joy and praise from all and sundry. As Reggie dribbles past four opponents, Ron, the defeated fullback, cries out 'Oh worthy opponent! Your skills have tormented me this afternoon but all credit to Reggie, the Welsh wizard!' All the supporters embrace each other after the game and cakes, twiglets and sausage rolls are guzzled as the party begins. The two rival managers crack open a bottle of champagne and offer a toast to the King of kings. God looks on and smiles. In this magical scenario the kingdom of God has just thrashed the kingdom of darkness by ten goals to nil.

Let us now imagine a very different world. Dour, faceless managers scream at their exhausted players. 'Get up that ******* wing and take that player out now!' Players torment each other with mocking grunts and scything tackles. Racist chants fill the stadium as hate-filled supporters throw banana skins on the pitch. Suddenly one of the goalkeepers clutches his bleeding face; someone has thrown a coin from the crowd. A fullback screams at his

own players. 'You ******* lazy ****. Work harder you
*****.' In this awful parallel universe the kingdom of
darkness has just thrashed the kingdom of God by ten
goals to nil. These two scenarios can help us in a beginning way to understand what Jesus meant by the kingdom of God.

When Jesus taught his disciples to pray he gave us
some important clues as to what this kingdom of God
might be like

> Our Father in heaven,
> hallowed be your name,
> your kingdom come,
> your will be done
> on earth as it is in heaven.
> Give us today our daily bread.
> Forgive us our debts,
> as we also have forgiven our debtors.
> And lead us not into temptation,
> But deliver us from the evil one.
>
> Matthew 6:9–13

In the first football scenario we see God's will being
done on earth. This is obviously connected to God's
kingdom. In the second scenario we see the total opposite. God's will is clearly not being done. Here then is a
crucial ingredient to the kingdom of God. We catch
glimpses of God's kingdom when we see footballers,
fans, managers, referees etc. doing God's will. But what
on earth might that mean? To understand this we need
to go back to the very first book in the Bible – Genesis.

1

Football and the Goodness of Creation

For many people today God has no interest in football. God is concerned with churches, hymns, pews, organs, flower arranging and heavenly visitations. God speaks in seventeenth century language and his focus is firmly upon eternal glories and realities. When we think of *religion* our thoughts turn to vicars, curates, vergers, fonts and collection plates. One day we will die and go to heaven and Jesus will offer us a heavenly hymn book and we will sing hymns for eternity. On this view football has almost nothing to do with Christianity. Football is frivolous and *worldly*. It might be helpful to kick a football around to keep fit and lose weight but playing football has no intrinsic value. True disciples of Christ are focused upon prayer, Bible study, souls and evangelism. Discussions about the relative merits of Chelsea and Manchester United do not elicit cries of joy and enthusiasm from such folk.

Many years ago, I remember mentioning to a fellow Christian that I enjoyed playing and watching football; I waxed lyrical about the elusive dribbling of George Best and the scorching piledrivers of Peter Lorimer. A lethal combination of disdain and pity invaded his normally cheerful demeanour. 'Brother Mark,' he whispered, 'I have no interest in such worldly amusements, the Lord has called me to higher things!'

On the other hand there are people who become obsessed with the game. They live, breathe and talk football incessantly. Spouses and children are often abandoned by these passionate disciples of the game. Every football fact is scrutinised and remembered. Huge sums of money are spent on football kits, football trips and football memorabilia. Obscure games in the Argentinian second division are viewed at three o'clock in the morning. The famous Liverpool manager Bill Shankly epitomised this approach to life when he declared

> Some people think football is a matter of life and death, I assure them it is much more serious than that.

It is almost as if football has become a form of pagan worship for some. We can imagine ancient people bowing down to rats, frogs, trees and crocodiles. And sometimes as football supporters bellow out their favourite songs and incantations, they seem similarly engaged.

But what does God think about the beautiful game? Is the Supreme Gaffer for or against it?

In order to grasp how God views football we need to understand the first two chapters of the book of Genesis. Let us summarise the central thrust of this story in three distinct phases. Firstly God creates the world out of nothing. We all know what it means when a striker is surrounded by four or five burly defenders and with consummate skill beats them all! A shimmy there, a drag-back here, and finally an explosive shot which leaves the net bulging. We often say that the striker made the goal from nothing. And that's what God did in the beginning. At first only God existed and then bang – the universe came into being. Awesome power and deft control. God speaks his word and the cosmos appears.

The second phase of Genesis is rather more complicated. God takes this uncrafted and undeveloped universe and he begins to shape and mould it. Just as a potter takes a lump of clay and then fashions it into a beautiful vase, so God brings order and wonderful diversity to this formless mass. On the first day darkness is distinguished from light, night from day. On the second day the waters above and below are separated. On the third day the lower waters are divided into dry land and sea, and then the land is filled with lush vegetation. On the fourth day God makes the lights appear in the sky, the moon, the sun and the stars. On the fifth day God fills the air and sea with birds and fishes. On the sixth day God makes humans and tells them to be fruitful and fill the earth. At the end of chapter 1 we are told that 'God saw all that he had made, and it was very good.' To put it in another way, 'Wow! What a cracker!'

This phase in the creation of the world can be compared to the visionary manager who arrives at a struggling third division club. He is appalled by the donkeys and blockheads who welcome him (the team). All the players hoof the ball up the park and seem more robotic than human. Turnip football reigns supreme. Derek Pilkington is determined to turn the club around. His best friend, Jack Dobson, is a multi-millionaire and, flush with cash, he buys a French player from Arsenal and a Brazilian player from Middlesbrough. These two players ooze class and style from every pore and they bring fresh tactics and new skills to the club. Slowly the team changes and develops. A young genius of a lad called George West emerges from the youth team and takes his place in the first team. The long ball tactic is abandoned and a passing, skilful game materialises. Within five years the team has won the European Cup. Imagine Derek holding the cup and basking in the adulation, the fans singing his praises and chanting his name. He has crafted a very good team and he is enormously chuffed with his work. Fantasy? I plead guilty as charged. And yet this ridiculous vignette can help us to understand how Yahweh formed and fashioned this extraordinary world we call our home.

Have you ever watched squirrels gathering nuts? Have you ever observed crocodiles lurking by the river bank? Consider for a moment the ostrich as she buries her head in the sand. And why on earth did God create armadillos, rhinos and duck-billed platypuses? Isn't all this too amazing for words? Scripture tells us that the Gaffer of gaffers took this shapeless void and crafted it into this bobbydazzler we still enjoy today. This Supreme Supremo made a belter of a cosmos and declared that it was very good.

Let us turn now to the third phase of creation. It might seem that the Boss had finished his work and downed tools. I remember so vividly working on a building site in London. All day long I dug ditches and delivered bricks to beefy men who often tormented me with their wicked Cockney humour. 'How's the boffin today?' they would sneer. 'Swallowed a dictionary?' It is not always easy being a public school boy in such harrowing circumstances. When five o'clock came, I was relieved and eager to escape that scene of sweat and humiliation.

And in a sense God did put his feet up and rested from his labours. His Majesty had worked very hard and we can sense his pleasure and contentment as he surveyed his gigantic construction – heaven and earth. It must have been a marvellous moment of relaxation and sheer delight. A day off seemed entirely appropriate.

But there was still a great deal of work to be done! As God inspected his handiwork, the Supreme Supremo became aware of the exciting possibilities that lurked in the bowels of his creation. There was so much more that could be done. Just as a football team can improve and mature, this amazing world could be developed and enhanced. But who would do it? The Boss enjoyed delegating responsibilities to created beings. He would need to entrust further creative assignments to one of his creatures. He needed a trusty lieutenant, a reliable steward. He needed a gifted and responsible manager who could take things forward.

Who could possibly fill this slot? Lions would be obvious candidates for the big job. They were very strong and aggressive. 'Nobody would kick sand in their eyes,' mused the Almighty. They would be noted for their teams' hard tackling ability but there was a distinct lack of intellectual ability. Big cats were poor in the white heat of examination performance. Their reading and writing abilities were notoriously feeble. Clearly they would struggle with the job specifications.

Eagles looked pretty impressive with their flying abilities and razor sharp vision. Yahweh had been impressed with their crafty trick of throwing their babies out of their nests and then swooping down several minutes later to catch the poor blighters before crashing into the ground. An excellent teaching device by which to coax lazy youngsters into the joys of flight! They would be great with the youth team – altogether an impressive curriculum vitae. But again eagles lacked imagination and flair. Their inability to speak languages with fully developed syntax and grammar was also mentioned as counting against their appointment.

Crocodiles offered considerable cunning, strength and determination. Yahweh had noted their patience and sublime acting skills as they pretended to be harmless logs floating innocently in the mighty rivers of Africa. Sudden speed of movement and raw power were impressive qualities that they would bring to the job. They could train goal poachers like Gary Lineker, who would suddenly spring to life and get their toe onto the low cross sending it scorching into the net. However, their tendency to inertia and sheer laziness did not impress. 'Idle loafers!' was a popular accusation.

So humans got the contract. It is we who have been entrusted with this challenging task. We are the managers, the stewards, the vice-regents of God's world. We have all the qualities, skills and flair that this job needs. We are God's co-workers as we develop, enhance and improve God's stunning creation.

Play and fun is welcome in God's garden

When we imagine and probe the kind of life that Adam and Eve enjoyed before the snake ensnared them we should distinguish four different activities that Yahweh called them to engage in. First there was work to be done. 'The Lord God took the man and put him in the Garden of Eden to work it and take care of it.' (Gen. 2:15).

God wanted humans to manage, to steward, to enhance his garden while at the same time protecting its integrity. Second, Yahweh was keen for his human creatures to rest and enjoy the healing balm of sleep. In Genesis 2 Adam has a pleasant snooze and during this siesta Yahweh creates his companion – Woman! We all know that sleep is essential to a healthy human life.

Third, Yahweh wanted his human creatures to worship him. It is good to sing to Yahweh and tell him how wonderful, powerful and glorious he is. Adam and Eve were probably very good at this and it is certain that they made a 'mighty noise unto the Lord'. Fourth, we need to notice that life in the garden provided ample opportunities for play, fun, laughter and jollification. Let us spend a few moments pondering this delightful pastime.

As Adam and Eve are exploring the garden, they begin to notice the vast range of trees on offer. 'Look over there my love,' coos the smitten Adam. 'Let's call that one a weeping willow.' Eve is over the moon with this clever appellation and beams her approval. 'Spotter's badge for the boy Adam.'

As they advance deeper into this wild and tree-infested part of the garden, they espy a banana tree and gently they pick two of these alluring fruits. Eve is particularly taken with this yellow dainty and she wolfs down the lush fruit. Adam is rather more restrained. 'I think I prefer those peaches we found yesterday to this amusement arcade.' Eve casually tosses the banana skins to one side as the two happy humans continue their voyage of discovery.

One hour later the couple are laughing and giggling as they return to this spot. Adam runs ahead of Eve and trips over the banana skins. Eve laughs like a cackling hyena and the first slapstick moment in history has been acted out. Many years later Brian Rix and Alan Ayckbourn would bring this form of comedy into thousands of unsuspecting theatres.

You may, like me, be unappreciative of this kind of comedy. Indeed both Jim Tickner and I do not relish this kind of humour. We tend to go more for biting satire and stinging irony. But the point is clear. Adam and Eve were learning to play and frolic in God's garden.

God created humans with a desire to play and muck about. Scripture affirms our craving for laughter and fun. There is room in God's world for horsing about and frivolous tomfoolery. Let's clarify what we mean when we talk about play.

Play defined

Sometimes it's very difficult to know how to distinguish between work and play. Paul Marshall, in his book *Heaven Is Not My Home*, offers us the following insight

> What is the spirit that distinguishes play? It's quite simple, though profound. *Play is what we do for no reason at all. Play is not done for any reason outside of itself. It is done for its own sake.*[2]

Play can be very energetic and exhausting. Mountain climbing is, for most of its devotees, a form of play and this is because mountain climbing is not done for any reason outside of itself. We know that traipsing up Mount Everest is dangerous and arduous and yet some people will pay serious sums of money in order to fulfil this longing. In sharp contrast when we ask a teacher why she is marking twenty-five essays on Polonius' relationship to Hamlet she will inform us that it has to be done. She must finish the task even though she is already exhausted. For this teacher marking books is work and in no sense can it be described as play.

Play is a gift from God. It is a freely chosen activity of fantasy for the purpose of having fun. Playful activity is saturated with secrets and surprises that await uncovering

---

[2] Paul Marshall, *Heaven Is Not My Home*, 108.

by a vivid imagination.[3] God's world radiates goodness and *joie de vivre*. And when we play we can bring honour to God. The Boss of bosses enjoys watching his creatures playing and making merry. This comes through very clearly in the book of Zechariah

> This is what the Lord says: 'I will return to Zion and dwell in Jerusalem. Then Jerusalem will be called the City of Truth, and the mountain of the Lord Almighty will be called the Holy Mountain.' This is what the Lord Almighty says: 'Once again men and women of ripe old age will sit in the streets of Jerusalem, each with cane in hand because of his age. The city streets will be filled with boys and girls playing there.'
>
> Zechariah 8:3–5

I remember the time I went to Stamford Bridge to watch Chelsea play the New York Cosmos. Two of the giants of the game, Cruyff and Rivelino, were there to entertain us. I still remember the look of total bafflement on Ron Harris' face when Cruyff performed his famous turn on the hapless defender. I was also entranced by Rivelino's ability to pass the ball. He would hit the ball very hard and you were certain that it must end up in the crowd. The crafty Brazilian had put so much back spin on the ball that at the last possible moment the ball stopped dead. Outrageous! God's glory is revealed to us in these unexpected moments of sheer playful audacity.

In conclusion we can affirm that God calls his human creatures to work, worship, rest and play in this world. That is what Adam and Eve were called to do and that is what we are called to do now. Football is just one of the many games that humans have unfolded as they have responded to God's call to develop and enhance his garden.

---

[3] Bradshaw Frey, *At Work and Play*, 43.

SATAN TEMPTS STRIKER.

2

Football and the Kingdom of Darkness

Football can be so fantastic. I remember playing football at school with my friends Alistair, Peter, Julian and Harry. Happy days! The laughter and banter were addictive and every game had tense moments of excitement and exhilaration. Julian's sliding tackles were truly gentle and good-humoured making us all giddy with mirth and delight. The dramatic joy and tension of those games will stay with me for the rest of my life, although my own lacklustre performances are best forgotten.

Several months ago I took my young son Emile (4) and my daughter Hannah (8) to a barbecue in Newport. Our friends Jimmy and Nicola Tottle had set up a tiny football pitch in their garden with two impressive goals. Greedily stuffing my fourth burger into my mouth, I furtively observed our children playing the game as they squealed and screamed with delight. Emile, the young nipper, scored a classic goal with a blistering toe-poke and throwing my burger aside I lunged into the local derby.

Within minutes I had plundered three goals and performed four drag-backs on the unsuspecting children. I beamed with pride as flashes of Eric Cantona's Wembley triumph surged through my mind. Just then Jimmy Tottle and his father Chris (nicknamed Sir Stanley) launched themselves into the unjust combat and before long all the adults and children were engrossed in this battle of the Titans. There was a girl playing who had broken her foot and she passed the ball with her crutch. She played really well and we all marvelled at her skill and finesse. What a day and what a match!

I remember thanking God for that game as we drove home together. I was humbled and moved by the experience; all the ingredients had gelled together perfectly on that barmy Saturday afternoon. Football, wine, burgers, children and good company.

One of my favourite passages in the Bible hints at the bliss and sheer pleasure associated with the kingdom of God. It's a total cracker and I therefore quote it in full.

> On this mountain the Lord Almighty will prepare a feast of rich food for all peoples, a banquet of aged wine – the best of meats and the finest of wines. On this mountain he will destroy the shroud that enfolds all peoples, the sheet that covers all nations; he will swallow up death for ever. The Sovereign Lord will wipe away the tears from all faces; he will remove the disgrace of his people from all the earth.
>
> Isaiah 25:6–8

Whilst I respect the forceful and commanding way in which Chris Tottle orchestrates the barbecue feast with his firm no-nonsense approach to the sausages and his deft handling of the charcoal, it will pale by comparison when the Lord Almighty dishes out the posh nosh on that mountain. What a day that will be! The kingdom of God will fill the earth and sadness and mourning will flee away. Jim and I will be the first people to remove our shirts and organise a football tournament. We will invite some of the smaller angels to join in on the strict understanding that they will not outshine us with their crisp passing and bullet-like headers. This would be going too far and in my opinion would create a redeemed rancour and resentment among the vast majority of players.

Football turns sour

But we know that football is often very different from these delightful scenarios. Have you ever opened a milk bottle, slurped it and discovered it was sour, with the bitter consistency of cottage cheese? Football can be a bit like that. Vitriol, petulance and spite seem endemic in this game we love. The famous Manchester United player Roy Keane has admitted in his autobiography that he deliberately set out to hurt an opponent with a vicious over-the-top tackle. Revenge was the motive, pure and simple. Tackling can be a skilful act of sublime theft but it can also degenerate into plain thuggery. And another famous player has complained that he is *only* earning £35,000 a week! We can only pity the poor lad as he struggles to make ends meet on that kind of salary! You do not need to be a world-famous brain surgeon to understand that football today is consumed by greed, selfishness and violence!

But why has the game gone so badly wrong? Why has the beautiful game turned so ugly? To understand this we need to understand the third chapter in the book of Genesis. Modern professional football is full of deals and contracts. Manchester United's famous manager Alex Ferguson is constantly buying and selling players. He is always on the lookout for talented new players and in the summer of 2002 he spent almost £30 million on the England defender Rio Ferdinand. When a big team like United sign a new player they discuss terms with the player and his agent. They agree upon a salary and the terms of employment. The club makes a promise and the player agrees to fulfil the terms of the contract. It was just like this at the very dawn of time.

In the very beginning God, as the Supreme Supremo of the cosmos, entered into a contract with his human creatures. He said: 'Obey me and you will live happily ever after. Disobey me and you will be miserable and eventually you will die.' As the supreme and all-powerful Gaffer, God had every right to make this kind of deal. In theological terms God entered into a covenant with Adam and Eve; this covenant or treaty contained both a promise and a threat. Obedience would lead to blessing and disobedience would lead to misery and alienation.

Lurking in the wings was another creature who was intrigued by the terms of this covenant. Lucifer, the fallen angel, was delighted to read the precise contents of the big deal and noticed that he could pull off the biggest transfer in the history of the cosmos. Satan realised that he could get hold of every human defender, midfield dynamo or striker through his own considerable cunning and sublime deceit. There was no need for a bung or extravagant transfer fees (e.g. £49 million for Zidane). Money would not be required as the Father of lies pressed home his deadly strategy.

'I'll take the woman first and then Adam will be mine,' mused the ugly, slimy snake. 'If I can force an early goal, the cup will be mine. If I pull this one off I'll win the World Cup every four years and all the best players (humans) will belong to me.'

This is, of course, a ridiculous and tongue in cheek reconstruction of how the devil conspired against God and the human race but it does help us to understand how men and women turned their backs on God and embraced the kingdom of darkness. It's instructive to notice that two covenants are powerfully at work. On the one hand the true King of the world issues his promises and his threats. Obedience will lead to life and blessing. Disobedience will lead to death and cursing. The false usurping king (Satan) is also busy making his promises. Humans will be rewarded if they reject their creator, and believe the serpent's crafty pleadings: 'Believe in me and you will be very happy and become as powerful as God.'

In a sense Adam and Eve were transferred to the worst possible club you could ever imagine. They signed on the dotted lines and it all went pear-shaped. Picture it – Rio Ferdinand is promised the beautiful mansion, the sleek Ferrari and the £3 million salary. He can't wait to begin; the contract looks so enticing! He turns up on his first day and he is commanded to clean mud-encased boots all day and toady to the big stars. His big salary is cancelled and he is paid £25 a week. His mansion turns out to be a hovel and his stylish Ferrari has transmogrified into a scruffy, yellow Fiesta. He has signed a new contract and failed to read the small print – it turns out to be a living nightmare.

We would understand perfectly if Rio seemed slightly perturbed and disappointed by this contractual betrayal. And that's exactly what Adam and Eve felt on that fateful day. Pain, grief, turmoil and overwhelming sadness. They were promised the moon and it turned out to be a rancid piece of festering gorgonzola! Mind you, they could hardly complain – they were warned, and they still made the wrong choice.

The Jewish prophet Isaiah can help us to understand the consequences of breaking covenant with Yahweh.

> The earth dries up and withers, the world languishes and withers, the exalted of the earth languish. The earth is defiled by its people; they have disobeyed the laws, violated the statutes and broken the everlasting covenant. Therefore a curse consumes the earth; its people must bear their guilt.
>
>   Isaiah 24:4–6a

It is vital to notice the all-pervading and radical nature of this curse. Turning our backs on the Gaffer of gaffers affects the entire created order. The ravages of sin and rebellion are spectacular and catastrophic. Let us investigate six crucial relationships that have become twisted and perverted by the fall.

1. God's relationship to humans has become fraught with pain and conflict. Before the rebellion, the Lord God had strolled about the garden in the cool of the day (Gen. 3:8). In some sense God's presence on the earth was visible, tangible and magnetic. Adam and Eve could chat and joke with the Almighty in a stress-free environment; the channels of communication were open and relaxed. But after the rebellion, God withdrew from the earth and retreated to heaven. Humans, from their side, can now experience God as distant and uninvolved. Communication with God becomes a struggle and some people can feel abandoned by God.

2. The relationship between humans is often consumed
   with loathing, bitterness and envy; a bit like the relationship between supporters of Spurs and Arsenal.
   Consider for a few moments the appalling acts of torture that are practised in hundreds of countries every
   year. Amnesty International has bravely alerted us to
   the savage brutality that befouls this planet.
   Remember the dreadful concentration camps at
   Auschwitz, Treblinka and Dachau where SS soldiers
   perpetrated unspeakable crimes against Jews,
   Gypsies and other 'undesirables'. We would also do
   well to remember that by the time that the slave trade
   had been abolished in Great Britain, some fifteen million African women, men and children had been
   taken as slaves. Out of this huge total, nine million
   had died in transit to other countries!

3. The relationship between women and men can be violent and abusive, and not just because the bloke wants
   to watch the England match instead of *Blind Date*!
   There is rape and sexual harassment; domestic violence and adultery. There are even stories of brothers
   who kill their sisters because they have flirted with
   unsuitable men. Men can sometimes bully women
   and women, in their turn, can become subservient,
   passive and manipulative. Prostitution is another part
   of this broken relationship. In Thailand there are
   tragic stories of fathers who sell their daughters to
   brothels for as little as the price of a fridge.

4. Rebellion against God has also affected our relationship with ourselves. This feature of the fall is often
   ignored and unexamined. It is very easy in a consumer-
   orientated society to dislike or even hate oneself. As we
   admire the beauty and grace of gorgeous film stars we

can become intensely irritated by our own physical imperfections and flaws. Despite the fact that famous and talented footballers appear to have everything going for them, we still hear stories of alcoholism, drug-addiction and other self-destructive behaviour. This insecurity has led to the enrichment of hundreds of plastic surgeons as they reshape and remodel cheeks, buttocks, noses and breasts. Further, anorexia and bulimia can haunt some peoples' lives and without doubt Hollywood seems to prefer scrawny, wraith-like actresses who diet with considerable venom. Numerous neuroses affect the human race.

5. The relationship between humans and animals has been spoiled and corrupted by the fall and this far more than the natural contempt we feel for those silly club mascots, the lions, foxes and chickens that prance about on the touchline of our football stadia. In the biblical story humans were supposed to look after the animals, birds and insects. We can catch glimpses of this even now as we watch a film like *Free Willy* which depicts the friendly and tender relationship between a young boy and a whale. The film also exposes the sheer greed that can captivate the human heart and the ruthless destruction of many sea creatures as humans sniff the smell of hard currency. At the same time crocodiles, lions and sharks take their revenge as they pounce on unsuspecting human beings. Although animals do not sin, they have been affected by the fall.

6. Finally the relationship between humans and the earth has been ravaged by sin and human rebellion, and this is far more serious than the dreadful state of the pitches in January. Humans were supposed to

lovingly cultivate the earth and enhance the superb garden that God had made. We were commanded to be stewards and friends of the earth but in our rebellion we have become violent and greedy molesters of the planet. Acid rain, pollution in our lakes and seas, the greenhouse effect – all these disturbing phenomena bear witness to our rebellion against God.

The ugly game in the dock

Last night I turned on the television and watched Manchester United playing an obscure Hungarian team in the Champions League. Somehow the whole experience left me feeling rather jaded and ill at ease. I became acutely aware that one set of players were being paid millions of pounds for playing the game and the other players were probably earning considerably less. I became sharply aware that for many people today football has become a substitute, pagan religion. The bitter consequences of sin and rebellion hurled themselves at me like a pack of demented jackals. I stood up, left the room and began to pray (but Manchester United still won!).

Perhaps that night I shared something of the apostle Paul's attitude when he wrote

> We know that the whole creation has been groaning as in the pains of childbirth right up to the present time. Not only so, but we ourselves, who have the firstfruits of the Spirit, groan inwardly as we wait eagerly for our adoption as sons, the redemption of our bodies.
>
> Romans 8:22,23

Football is sick and in urgent need of a doctor. Violence and hatred seem omnipresent. Some football fans sing appalling things about David Beckham's wife Victoria and their young sons Brooklyn and Romeo. The taunts and screams of some fans are repulsive and repellent. Grown men utter profanities and vulgarities as their young children drink in the poisoned atmosphere of a yobbish and often racist football culture. In Glasgow there is unceasing hostility between Celtic and Rangers fans; a young fan was recently stabbed to death because he was wearing a Rangers football shirt. Millwall's odious F-troop leave calling cards on the unconscious bodies of their victims: 'You have just been serviced by F-troop' is their 'witty' catchphrase.

Greed stalks the game in Jack the Ripper fashion. Some players are earning more than £5 million a year and, as we noted earlier, there are players who are deeply aggrieved that they are forced to make do on far less. The Colombian striker Faustino Asprilla has stated that he cannot play for a particular club because he cannot make ends meet on the humble weekly £17,000 he was to be paid! A recent survey by Il Sole-24 Ore (Italy's equivalent of the *Financial Times*) demonstrated that professional clubs (Serie A down to C2) had a total operating loss of £654,570 million for the year ending June 2001, with clubs like Ternana (now in Serie C1) paying out as much as 183 per cent of their turnover in salaries![4]

The price of replica football kits has also sparked off intense debate about greed in the game. Football shirts cost about £7 to make and yet they retail for about £40! Someone is making a very healthy profit. During the World Cup in Japan, replica tops of teams taking part in the tournament were being sold for £80 to £100! Clubs now cynically redesign their home and away strip on a

---

[4] I am indebted to the September 2002 issue of the football magazine *When Saturday Comes* for these shocking statistics.

regular basis, forcing avid fans and harassed parents to shell out yet again for the new strip.

For some people today football has become a form of pagan religion. In the ancient world, people would worship trees, rivers and even rats. In the modern world there are those who make football into a false god. There are tragic stories of women who have divorced their husbands on the grounds that they have become *football widows*. There are some people who become so obsessed by the game that they spend all their money and all their time on this particular activity. This is the bitter fruit of sin and rebellion against God.

We must also consider the aesthetic dimension of football. We have argued that football is a form of play and in this humble context can indeed bring glory to God. Football should encourage spontaneity, innovation and joy in the unexpected. Too often, however, football can become one-dimensional, functional and monotonous. It is instructive to observe certain coaches who induce fear and anxiety in their young charges. 'Get rid!! Get rid!!' they scream. A player who tries an audacious trick is reprimanded and rebuked with considerable venom. This can easily create the kind of player who is extremely fit and strong but who lacks both vision and technique. In footballing terms *turnip* football begets *donkeys*, only capable of hoofing the ball up the pitch. This lack of aesthetic richness is also part of the fall.

Sometimes in my darker moments, when I consider the festering boils, pustules, carbuncles and warts that have enveloped this wonderful game, I become sorrowful, disenchanted and sullen. Perhaps football has become too bad and too sick. Perhaps those who hate the game are right. Perhaps those of us who love God and love football are wrong.

3

Football and God's Law

Imagine a mysterious virus has devastated the planet and very few people have survived. The remnant has found each other and huddle together in a large church on the outskirts of Watford in the county of Hertfordshire. They are all thrilled to discover that they are all seasoned and mature disciples of Jesus Christ and they launch into spontaneous praise and worship. The joy and gladness of the assembled throng is irresistible and before long enthusiastic discussions about the kingdom of God break out like a raging fever. Derek, the former plumber, impresses the congregation with his expert knowledge on the book of Ephesians and Sally, the former air hostess, sparkles as she unleashes her honeyed insights about the book of Ecclesiastes. Gareth Owens, a former miner from Wales, belts out his poignant and dramatic interpretation of 'Bread of Heaven' and Tina Tuffty, a former surgeon from Leeds, accompanies him on the cello. The remnant is spellbound and pleads passionately with Gareth to sing the great classic again and again.

Suddenly and rather rudely, Don McCalpine, a rather dour Scotsman from Aberdeen, punctures the atmosphere with a sharp and penetrating insight. 'It's all very well singing and whooping it up like Bruce Forsyth in a Royal Variety Performance but have you thought about the pointlessness and misery of our condition! I mean there are no heathens and atheists to evangelise, so what on earth are we going to do with the rest of our lives?'

Joy ebbs away as theological reflection turns sour. The congregation had been so happy for so many hours and now the bitter truth of Don's brief homily elicits moaning and groaning in the chastened assembly. Sally stands up and declares ruefully:

'Don's right. There's no point being here. All our souls are saved. I wish I could die now and go straight to heaven.'[5]

Would we agree with Don and Sally that life under these conditions would become pointless and miserable? What exactly have Don and Sally failed to understand? Have they understood the message of the Bible?

We have tried to point out in this book that God has given us a task to perform. Theologians sometimes refer to this as the cultural mandate. In the beginning God told us to cultivate and care for his garden. We suggested that this task embraces obedient work, rest and play. God calls us to enhance and develop his garden. Football is just one of the many responses that we can make to our God and King.

Even though we sin and turn against God, we are still called to develop and unfold this wonderful world. We cannot help but do it. We carry on camping (Gen. 4:20). We carry on raising livestock (Gen. 4:20). We carry on playing harps and flutes (Gen. 4:21). We carry on making tools of bronze and iron (Gen. 4:22). We carry on watching ridiculous films starring Sid James, Kenneth

---

[5] We are indebted to Richard Russell for the original idea for this story.

Williams and Charles Hawtrey. We carry on playing cricket, rugby and Gaelic football. We just can't help it because that's the way we're made. God made us creative, imaginative and intelligent creatures. That's what we folks do!

In footballing terms we don't stop being managers after the fall. We carry on being managers even if we do the job wretchedly and sinfully. The mandate given to Adam and Eve, and through them to us, has not ended. But we have failed to follow it in loving, responsive and life-giving ways. We carry out the same tasks, but we perform these tasks in evil and corrupt ways.[6]

God in his mercy and grace comes to restore and redeem our lives and our development of the garden. He doesn't say – stop trading, stop building houses, stop making music and stop playing and having fun. Rather Yahweh says – carry on doing these things but do it – My Way. In this sense we can learn some excellent theology from the Frank Sinatra classic, although it would be rash to assume that Mr Sinatra intended such pedagogical insight.

We could say that in the first book of the Bible (Genesis) we discover what God has called us to do and in the second book of the Bible (Exodus) we discover how we are to go about this task. The book of Exodus contains the laws that God revealed to Moses. They are instructive about many things and their implications for the beautiful game will be explored.

God's Law

We gain considerable insight into God's purposes for the world when we study the Mosaic Law. You can find

---

[6] We are indebted to Paul Marshall for this insight.

these laws in the books of Exodus, Leviticus, Numbers and Deuteronomy. Many people are surprised to learn that Real Madrid have won the European Cup nine times and such folk are often also surprised to learn that the Mosaic Law includes more than 600 laws. Surely, they carp, these figures must be too high! It is a popularly held belief that God gave Moses ten and only ten of those famous commandments. Wrong.

We all know how important it is to understand the rules of football. Imagine a game where half the players have failed to grasp the basic rules and regulations. Ricky is haring down the wing and suddenly picks the ball up with his left hand. Frank decides to score goals at the wrong end and Chippy tackles people by squirting lemon juice into their eyes. Nosejob refuses to remove his ferrets from his shorts and Bluebeard keeps kicking the ball as high as he can into the adjacent wood. We can all agree that this would be bedlam. Anarchy would reign and football would become impossible.

The Supreme Gaffer is keenly aware that life on this planet becomes impossible when humans fail to respect certain rules of conduct. We are creatures who urgently require guidance and instruction from the Boss. It was in this context that God revealed his law to Moses.

We must now investigate some of the key laws and relate them to the game of football. We will select some basic fundamental laws that communicate the spirit and thrust of God's word.

Jubilee

When we investigate modern football clubs we soon realise that there is a massive difference in income between the top clubs and the minnows of the game. Teams like Scunthorpe and Boston United struggle to make ends meet whereas the giants of the game (Manchester United, Arsenal and Liverpool) will buy players for fantastic sums of money. There is, in short, massive inequality of wealth; there is also very little guesswork needed to predict the recipients of future silverware!

The Mosaic Law would take issue with this parlous state of affairs. The Supreme Gaffer made it very clear to Moses that each Israelite family was to be given an inheritance of land. It was crucial to keep each family connected to its portion of real estate. Not only could each and every family grow their food and enjoy the bread, meat, sauces and condiments essential to fine living but ample opportunities for play and relaxation would be guaranteed. The land of Israel did not belong to fat cats and greedy tycoons. The land belonged to God and he rented it out equally to all his people.

The Guvnor explained to Moses that team tactics should always give every family at least four or five touches during live matches. In other words if any family had lost its land for whatever reason, they should return to their estate at the year of Jubilee which would happen once in every fifty years. You can read about this in Leviticus 25. (You would be ill-advised to read this chapter if you manage any of the top clubs in Europe.)

The economic consequences of this law would tend to prevent some families becoming very rich and other families becoming very poor. At the year of Jubilee the rich would get poorer and the poor would get richer. It doesn't require a degree in Economics to grasp how this law is relevant to the modern game.

Sabbath rest

We encounter a similar law in the book of Deuteronomy. The Supreme Gaffer pointed out that the Jubilee law was most excellent and efficacious in preventing the fat cat-starving mouse kind of game. Waxing lyrical, the Guvnor explained further tactics to the by now middle-aged and balding Moses. 'Every seven years we will abandon the normal league system and go for something really novel. In this seventh year we will cancel all debts, release all slaves and have a holiday for one year!'

Moses gasped at the sheer effrontery of the Guvnor's tactical suggestions. 'What do you mean, Boss?' yelped the former Egyptian journeyman. We all understand how some footballers' eyes become glazed and inattentive when loquacious managers expound difficult and complicated tactics. And this might have been the response of Moses but not for long.

God explained to the humble lad (Num. 12:3) his precise intentions. 'All professional, money-focused activities must stop for one year in seven. All people and animals must rest and the land as well. It's for your own good! Rest and relaxation are crucial ingredients in my philosophy. You can play football in the year off but not for money!'

The precise instructions contained in Deuteronomy 15 are remarkably radical. Rich people must cancel debts to poor, vulnerable people, they must set slaves free and stop all economic activities for an entire year. Strikingly the text declares that

> However, there should be no poor among you, for in the land the Lord your God is giving you to possess as your inheritance, he will richly bless you, if only you fully

obey the Lord your God and are careful to follow all
these commands I am giving you today.

Deuteronomy 15:4,5

This Sabbath year law strikes a painful and sharp blow
to the greed and avarice that oppresses the beautiful
game. Players who are driven to work too hard and then
complain of tiredness at the World Cup should marinade in the wisdom of the Sabbath. Avaricious clubs
which refuse to take a break from economic activity
should ponder afresh the wonder of God's instruction.
Too much money and too much work cripple and ham-
string human creatures. Consider the relevance of
Exodus to the modern game

> For six years you are to sow your fields and harvest the
> crops, but during the seventh year let the land lie
> unploughed and unused. Then the poor among your
> people may get food from it, and the wild animals may
> eat what they leave. Do the same with your vineyard
> and your olive grove. Six days do your work, but on the
> seventh day do not work, so that your ox and your don-
> key may rest and the slave born in your household, and
> the alien as well, may be refreshed.
>
> Exodus 23:10–12

This passage resonates with themes of stewardship and
refreshment. We are reminded of the cultural mandate
as the Mosaic Law addresses our husbandry of animals
and land. We should be struck by God's urgent plea that
the entire created order should learn to enter God's rest.
Funnily enough the more we trust in God, the more we
discover rest, recreation and the delights of play! We
would do well to understand that the Mosaic Law
earnestly enjoins us to find a healthy rhythm of work,

rest, play and worship. Let us turn now to another important theme in the Law.

Feasting and celebration

Last year when Jim Tickner won his first piece of proper silverware in the Bristol Church League, we were all chuffed for the lad and a party seemed appropriate. To be completely accurate it needs to be pointed out that Jim seemed rather smug as he bathed in the congratulations and good will of the assembled throng. He positively gloated as he regaled his wife and pals with the glories and sacrifices of that hard-fought campaign. I checked to see if Jim had a shadow and I was not surprised when there was none to be seen.

We all have moments in our lives when a feast or celebration cries out for frenzied activity. Tim Bowman (a plucky pal of ours) is often commissioned to bring the twiglets. Lou Tickner (spouse of Jim) is dispatched to purchase the pork scratchings and Su Bowman is ordered on pain of death to bring copious quantities of lager beer. I make the lasagne and the salad while my wife Anne sits on the sofa and rebukes us for our sloth and negligence. Such are the delights of a well-earned feast.

It was no different at the time of Moses. Here is a typical passage in the book of Deuteronomy

> Use the silver to buy whatever you like: cattle, sheep, wine or other fermented drink, or anything you wish. Then you and your household shall eat there in the presence of the Lord your God and rejoice.
>
> Deuteronomy 14:26

Feasting, celebrating and rejoicing before the face of God are constant reminders to us that the biblical God enjoys watching his people having a serious and committed knees-up. God's world radiates goodness and extravagance – dancing, partying and mucking about can be redeemed. We are not speaking here about a sordid and seedy event but something that is wholesome and pleasing to God.

Laws about gleaning and concern for the marginalised

One of the most intriguing laws in the book of Leviticus concerns the activity known as gleaning

> When you reap the harvest of your land, do not reap to the very edges of your field or gather the gleanings of your harvest. Do not go over your vineyard a second time or pick up the grapes that have fallen. Leave them for the poor and the alien. I am the Lord your God.
>
> Leviticus 19:9,10

Can we imagine a farm where asylum seekers and beggars are allowed to join in with the picking of apples and pears? Instead of being shunned and avoided they are welcomed with open arms. The farm labourer is obliged to work far fewer hours because they must leave a substantial part of the crop untouched and ignored. Wounded, vulnerable men, women and children can enjoy a substantial part of the harvest. This theme is repeated in other parts of the Mosaic Law.

> At the end of every three years, bring all the tithes of that year's produce and store it in your towns, so that the

Levites (who have no allotment or inheritance of their own) and the aliens, the fatherless and the widows who live in your towns may come and eat and be satisfied, and so that the Lord your God may bless you in all the work of your hands.

Deuteronomy 14:28,29

The Old Testament refers very frequently to widows, orphans and foreigners and enjoins us to be generous, tender and open-hearted to such folk. Now that we have some cursory understanding of the Old Testament Law we can suggest the following football vignette which will help us to understand football in a new and fresh way.

Comical football vignette

Ronaldo was walking along the streets of Rio de Janeiro one fine day. He had just been awarded the Golden Boot for his eight goals in the World Cup final and he was over the moon. The previous evening he and Roberto Carlos had been studying the book of Leviticus in their weekly Bible study and Ronaldo had nutmegged Roberto on several occasions with his studious grasp of the selected passages. Carlos had looked so furtive and ill-equipped as the world's most famous player displayed his impressive biblical erudition.

Just then seven homeless orphans came into view. Ronaldo smiled as the ragamuffins bellowed and screamed their delight and approval. 'Ronaldo, Ronaldo,' they chanted in unison. Just then Roberto Carlos sauntered up clutching seven ice creams and offered them to the children. 'Still smarting from last night?' beamed the World's Greatest Player. 'Huh!' mumbled the sullen Carlos.

'Let's get down to a serious game of footie with these lads,' Ronaldo suggested and patted the left-back affectionately on the shoulder. 'Show these lads your ferocious bender.' 'Yes, yes, go on Roberto, do your thing,' shouted the orphans. Carlos' irritable demeanour visibly melted as the game exploded into intense activity. Two hours later the happy group decided to hold an impromptu prayer session; they were all sweating and exhausted from the furious pace of the game. Ronaldo could not wait to share his good news.

'You lads are not going to believe this but I've managed to find your parents and they will be arriving shortly. I've paid off all their debts and they are no longer bonded slaves working two hundred miles away for that evil rogue Señor Oliveras de Santos. They are free and looking forward to our party tonight!' The boys were speechless. 'Oh and by the way,' chipped in the smiling and emotionally rejuvenated Carlos, 'Ronaldo and I have bought a couple of houses for you and your parents and your careers as waifs and strays are now officially terminated.'

The Mosaic Law opens our eyes to the kingdom of God. If humans hear what God is saying through his word they cannot fail to be impressed. When people respond faithfully to God's word we begin to glimpse what the Bible calls shalom. Shalom refers to exciting scenarios which breathe peace, justice and good will. We will speak more of this crucial concept in the next chapter.[7]

---

[7] We are indebted to Bob Goudzwaard for many of the ideas in this chapter.

4

Football and Shalom

It often comes as a shock to some people just how much money some football players are earning. Alan Shearer is now worth £17 million and David Beckham is reported to have earned about £10 million last year. His salary at Manchester United is only a part of his total earnings; he has extremely lucrative contracts with Adidas and Brylcream which top up his earnings. Becks owns seven cars including a custom built Ferrari, a Porsche 911, a Range Rover and a Jaguar. David and his wife Victoria own a magnificent mansion in Hertfordshire and a luxurious flat in Alderley Edge. When they go shopping, they can buy pretty much what they want and it is unlikely that they shop in Kwik Save or Somerfield. Some football players are very shrewd with their cash and are able to retire at a young age with vast fortunes. Others are not so circumspect. George Best summed up his attitude to money and life when he remarked: 'I spent a lot of my money on booze, birds and fast cars. The rest I just squandered.'

It also comes as quite a shock to some people that slavery still exists today! The Anti-Slavery Society contends that there are some 200 million people in the world today who are living and working in circumstances that can only be described as slavery. This figure is far higher than when slavery was abolished in the second half of the nineteenth century! In some countries there are slaves who are owned by slave masters who have inherited them via a *debt* carried over from their deceased parents and grandparents. They earn no money, so they can never pay off these illusory debts. In remote parts of the Philippines children are born into slavery and whole families are traded for as little as £60. For as little as the price of a replica shirt you can actually buy a person in some parts of the third world!

One of the most vivid images of redemption in the Old Testament concerns the purchase of a slave by a close relative. This kinsman-redeemer would sometimes travel long distances in order to rescue one of his cousins, aunties or uncles from a life of bonded slavery. He would approach the slave master, cash in hand, and buy the person back. This is the root meaning of the word *redeem*. In football, famous players are bought for millions of pounds and are then paid millions of pounds by the clubs that employ them. Perhaps we could say rather provocatively that the kingdom of God has indeed come when wealthy footballers spend more money on releasing slaves than buying Ferraris.

God's Law is still enormously relevant to our modern world. Obedience to this law would bring shalom to the world. Shalom is far more than peace and absence of conflict; it is wholeness, completeness, perfection and security in every area of creation, and every area of personal, social, intellectual and artistic life. And in the wholeness and flourishing of shalom, all these areas of life are inundated with joy and rejoicing. Picture a world where everything functions beautifully and according to God's will. That's shalom. It wouldn't be so bad, would it?[8]

Israel was supposed to be a land filled with kinsman-redeemers. Israel was called by God to make his presence visible, magnetic and tangible. Israel had the task of making God feel at home on the earth. God wanted to live with his human creatures and walk in the cool of the day with them. God was nostalgic for the old days when he talked face to face with Adam and Eve. The God who is normally invisible longs to become visible (flesh and blood) and broadcast the good news of his kingdom loud and clear to anyone who might listen.

Shalom during the reign of Solomon

And we could say that this almost happened some three thousand years ago. We catch a glimpse of this shalom during the reign of David's son Solomon, the third king of Israel. Let's explore what it was like to live in Israel during the early reign of Solomon. The book of Kings gives us some helpful information about this historical period.

Perhaps we should come clean right from the start. There is no evidence that anybody played football back in those far distant times. There was no Champions League and nobody had heard of Manchester United, Arsenal or Chelsea. People at the court of Solomon did not discuss the relative merits of Figo, Zidane, Ronaldo, Scholes, Beckham or Giggs. Certainly nobody complained that Real Madrid had poached all the best players and nobody did impressions of Alan Hanson or Gary Lineker. But should any of those players find themselves in a time

---

[8] I am indebted to Karen DeMol for this definition of shalom.

machine with an affable and co-operative Dr Who, they would be chuffed to find themselves whisked back to the glory days of Big Sol.

Solomon was a ruler who could have entertained our football heroes in style. His banquets and feasts were famous for their exotic cuisine of deer, gazelles, roebucks and choice fowl (1 Kgs. 4:23). Solomon's yearly income was huge; he pulled in more than 22 tons of gold every year (1 Kgs. 10:14)! We might even say that David Beckham would have seemed a pauper in comparison with Big Sol.

So often in the modern world great luxury comes at the cost of human squalor and degradation. We live in a world of outrageous contrasts; rich people are pampered and spoilt with their expensive Gucci adornments while the poor suffer enormous pain and privation. In Brazil it is estimated that there are between seven million and eleven million homeless people! It was not like this at the court of Solomon.

The book of Kings tells us that the Israelites lived comfortably and safely; each family enjoyed its inheritance from God. Everyone possessed land, vineyards and fig-trees (1 Kgs. 4:25). Further we are told that people ate and drank and were happy. There were no landless peasants who could be bought and sold at the drop of a hat. Peace and justice filled the land and happiness did not come at someone's expense.

We are also told that Solomon possessed great wisdom and insight. This is how 1 Kings puts it

> He was wiser than any other man, including Ethan the Ezrahite – wiser than Heman, Calcol and Darda, the sons of Mahol. And his fame spread to all the surrounding nations. He spoke three thousand proverbs and his songs numbered a thousand and five. He described plant life, from the cedar of Lebanon to the hyssop that

grows out of walls. He also taught about animals and birds, reptiles and fish. Men of all nations came to listen to Solomon's wisdom, sent by all the kings of the world, who had heard of his wisdom.

1 Kings 4:31–34

The early reign of Solomon was distinctive and impressive. Big Sol was responding to the cultural mandate with real style and panache. Not for him the life of the idle hedonist – loafing around the palace, loitering with intent, on the prowl for sordid pleasures. No; Big Sol was a cultured man. He understood God's call to develop and enhance the radiant garden. He spent time writing songs and proverbs. He studied all kinds of fascinating things – trees, animals, birds and insects. He was perhaps the first world-famous Educationalist, Composer, Botanist and Zoologist all rolled into one. People from all over the world heard about this dazzling king and his amazing kingdom and they booked their holidays and prepared their caravans.

The Queen of Sheba had heard about the fame of Solomon and decided to pay him a visit. We all know people who are inclined to over-pack; some people just can't seem to help it. We are told that she brought camels carrying spices, large quantities of gold, and precious stones (1 Kgs. 10:2). The precise weight of the gold should cause us some concern for her caravan; apparently it weighed 4 tons!

It's very easy to be overwhelmed by the sheer class of the present Real Madrid team. It would seem as if they've gained access to Solomon's vast fortune and have bought up the world's most costly players. Sheba was similarly overwhelmed on meeting Big Sol. She was deeply impressed by the shalom and magnificence that pervaded his court and kingdom. Her keen eye had alerted her to the dramatic contrast between Solomon's kingdom and all the other kingdoms she had visited as a young princess. Here there was no obvious misery, cruelty and oppression. Here there was wealth and stylish living but it was enjoyed by all the cheerful and affable citizens. Wisdom, human flourishing and festive celebration seemed omnipresent and Sheba gasped and gulped in fresh supplies of oxygen. 'What a corker,' she must have concluded.

Sheba was no slouch in matters of discernment herself. Clearly Solomon had waxed lyrical as he launched into literary, scientific, philosophical and theological disquisitions. Perhaps Sheba found Big Sol attractive and alluring; perhaps she fancied the dazzling charmer. Who knows? The Bible is sadly quiet on such matters. But on one important topic we can be crystal clear – Sheba realised that all this wonder and glory did not emanate from Solomon alone. Behind the throne stood someone else. This is how Sheba put it herself

> The report I heard in my own country about your achievements and your wisdom is true. But I did not believe these things until I came and saw with my own eyes. Indeed, not even half was told me; in wisdom and wealth you have far exceeded the report I heard. How happy your men must be! How happy your officials, who continually stand before you and hear your wisdom! Praise be to the Lord your God, who has delighted in you and placed you on the throne of Israel. Because of the Lord's eternal love for Israel, he has made you king, to maintain justice and righteousness.
>
> 1 Kings 10:6–9

We could say that Sheba glimpsed the presence of God as she observed the life of Israel. God was no longer invisible, unapproachable and intangible. She sensed the reality and power of God as she bathed and luxuriated in the shalom of Solomon's kingdom. For perhaps the first time in her life Sheba, the pagan queen, caught a glimpse of the kingdom of God and it elicited her praise and worship.

And yet this manifestation of the kingdom of God was to be so fleeting and ephemeral. Just as modern professional football has become twisted and corrupted by greed, violence and a win-at-all-costs mentality, so Solomon betrayed the God who had brought him so much fame, wealth and honour. In his old age Solomon became a seedy and sordid monarch, obsessed by the size of his harem and the strength of his armies.

I have often been struck by the parallels between the lives and careers of Solomon and the mercurial Manchester United footballer George Best. In his prime, Best was a dazzling and mesmeric player. He was the supreme entertainer and his talent embraced dribbling, passing, instant ball control, nutmegging, scoring, slide tackling, jumping, heading, riding hospital tackles and doing the unexpected. He would torment hapless defenders by beating them, stopping in mid-flight and beat them again! He incarnated the beautiful game. He was also very handsome, witty and charming. He won a European Cup medal with Manchester United in 1968 and was described by Pele as the most gifted natural player he had ever seen.

A well-known story about Bestie will help us to appreciate this glaring symmetry. A bell-boy happened to stroll into Best's hotel room where the great man was entertaining two beautiful young women. Several bottles of champagne were being consumed by the merry throng and a night's winnings from the local casino was scattered casually around the luxury suite. The bell-boy, it is said, asked the playboy, 'But George, where did it all go wrong?' Bestie is alleged to have gestured around the room and quipped ironically, 'You tell me, son.'

I think Solomon was prone to exactly the same weakness of character as George Best. Indeed the book of Kings tells us that he had seven hundred wives of royal birth and three hundred concubines. We are also told that his wives encouraged him to worship the pagan gods Chemosh, Molech and Ashtoreth. There is even the possibility that Solomon attended pagan festivals where human beings were sacrificed to these gods.

Evil hides the kingdom of God and Sheba would have been aghast to have encountered Solomon in his twilight years. A just and righteous king had become an ageing, leering playboy. Something very good had become something very bad.

Although we catch a few intoxicating moments of shalom in the history of Israel, too often the people rebelled against their divine calling and embraced the violence and corruption of pagan religion. Both Israel and football have flirted repeatedly with the false gods of money, sex and power. The kingdom of God has so often been suffocated and asphyxiated by the presence of evil and corruption.

The Prince of Shalom

The great prophets of the Old Testament reminded the Israelites of their repeated failures. They spoke about God's anger and disappointment with the ugliness and idolatry that besmirched his chosen people. Isaiah seethed with indignation and ranted and raved against the covenant people. We have all heard of managers who turn the air blue as they hurl teacups around the dressing room; incandescent with rage and fury as they castigate their players with the follies of poor passing and ignominious tackling. The famous manager Sir Alex Ferguson is renowned for this. He has even been dubbed 'the hairdryer' by some of his unfortunate charges!

Although Isaiah lived in a different time from the Manchester United supremo, he would have been sympathetic with the gaffer's spleen and displeasure. Isaiah was, at times, apoplectic with rage. Listen to this blast from the ancient Hebrew

> Woe to you who add house to house and join field to field till no space is left and you live alone in the land. The Lord Almighty has declared in my hearing: 'Surely the great houses will become desolate, the fine mansions left without occupants. A ten-acre vineyard will produce only a bath of wine, a homer of seed only an ephah of grain.' Woe to those who rise early in the morning to run after their drinks, who stay up late at night till they are inflamed with wine. They have harps and lyres at their banquets, tambourines and flutes and wine, but they have no regard for the deeds of the Lord, no respect for the work of his hands. Therefore my people will go into exile for lack of understanding ...
>
> Isaiah 5:8–13a

Isaiah is rebuking a generation of men and women who hedonistically cavorted in their luxurious mansions oblivious to the distressing cries of the landless peasants, the bonded slaves and the homeless orphans. This scenario is the polar opposite of Hebraic shalom and Isaiah does not mince his words. There are many parallels between the world of football and the world of Isaiah.

Isaiah does not only strike this sombre and soulful tone. He alludes on many occasions to a future permanent state of shalom and we must explore this for a few moments. The Hebrew hairdryer speaks about the coming of a 'Wonderful Counsellor, Mighty God, Everlasting Father, Prince of Peace.' This anointed servant will bring shalom and liberation to a groaning, moaning world. Isaiah offers us a wonderful picture of a restored and rejuvenated world where wolves live with lambs, leopards befriend goats and cows will feed with bears! Strikingly a little child will lead all these animals in a gentle procession. Vulnerable toddlers will play by a cobra's hole and no harm will come to them (Is. 11)! This servant of the Lord will turn the desert into an oasis and bring water into the parched wilderness. He will open the eyes of the blind and unblock the ears of the deaf. The lame will leap like the deer and the tongue of the speechless will shout for joy (Is. 35). What Sheba had glimpsed for a brief and shallow moment, this person would bring forever.

How then could God's shalom come to football? How could the rule of God invade that sphere of life we call football? Could we envision rich, powerful clubs sharing their huge resources with the minnows of the game? Is it possible to dream of football matches where winning-at-all-costs is no longer an acceptable philosophy? Can we imagine a world where footballers and their agents have become kinsman-redeemers?[9]

---

[9] We are indebted to Brian Walsh for his discussion about the importance of imagination in his excellent book *Subversive Christianity*.

5

Football and Misleading Conceptions of the Kingdom of God

Howard had retired from the professional game at the age of thirty-six. For several seasons he had endured the taunts of the younger players who often referred to him as *grandad* and the *ancient one*. His girth had expanded as he responded enthusiastically to the lavish cuisine of Bertha, his third (trophy) wife. Cries of *Old Tubby* and *Porky* did not console him in his final swansong season. Howard had not exerted himself at school and had resisted all attempts by each and every teacher to activate in him a lust for knowledge and learning. It could be stated without any equivocation that Howard had never finished a book in his entire life; his literary appreciation was poor and malnourished. When Eric Cantona spoke of his passion for the French poet Rimbaud, Howard had been convinced that the great French player had been referring to Rambo, the muscular character made famous by the Hollywood actor Sylvester Stallone. Howard decided, on the termination of his contract, to become a professional football manager. Clearly he would need to master the tactical nuances of the game.

He devoured the writings and literary output of Charles Hughes and became a disciple of the long ball game. Hughes had argued that most goals (87 per cent) are scored after five consecutive passes or less; when attacking, teams should go forward as quickly as possible. This philosophy of football is sometimes referred to as kick and rush.

Howard had achieved considerable success with small-town teams and now found himself the manager of Aston Villa. Popular with his players, Howard enjoyed the banter and badinage of the dressing-room and the occasional game of cards. After his first season, Aston Villa was drawn to play Bologna in the UEFA Cup first round. His assistant Bertie Travers impressed upon Howard the vital importance of preparation and the urgent need to study the opposing team with relentless and unswerving attention to detail. Howard dismissed Bertie's promptings with a contemptuous wave of his hand. Needless to say Aston Villa lost 3-0 in both home and away legs of the tie and Howard was sacked and replaced by Bertie Travers. Howard is now a postman working in Ruislip.

This football parable should alert us to the importance of understanding the opposition. Arsene Wenger, Gerard Houllier, Sir Alex Ferguson and Jim Tickner are keen students of the game and they all take time and care to ferret out the strengths and weaknesses of their opponents. We will now examine four perspectives on football and the kingdom of God that I believe to be utterly bankrupt and misleading.

The kingdom of God refers to souls going to heaven

Thousands of years ago a man called Plato was born in Greece. Unlike Howard, Plato excelled in reading, writing and spelling and before long he had consumed vast forests of knowledge and erudition. He had an unslakable lust for study and reflection and he refused to fritter away his youth on the ignominious pleasures of snooker, public houses and darts. Not for him the idle loafing of the criminal classes or the petulant struttings of the football hooligan. Far from it; Plato surrendered to the joys and agonies of intense intellectual exertion; his mind brimmed and cascaded with honeyed insights and probing forays into distant corners of the universe. His ferocious intellect locked onto abstract complexities like a barracuda chasing its prey; his agile mind seized on logical errors like a white shark gorging on some unfortunate seal. Plato was, without doubt, the George Best of the ancient academic world. He dazzled and shimmered with brilliance.

One of the great football debates focuses upon the precise identity of the world's greatest player of all time. Who is this fellow? Only four candidates are routinely submitted for public examination. They are Pele, Maradona, Johan Cruyff and George Best. Jim Tickner invariably plumps for Johan Cruyff and I normally go for Maradona. The arguments that we proffer for our candidates need not detain us here. I only mention this so as to buttress my contention that when we debate who was the greatest Greek philosopher, we should not embrace the folly of our football punditry. In football we can debate this eternal question with earnest conviction and sober intent but this becomes comical and mildly obscene when we debate the Greek question. It is laughable and contemptible to even suggest that Plato is not the supreme guvnor of the Greek intellectual milieu. Aristotle and Plotinus, worthy minds that they possessed, are not even in the same ball park as the noble Plato.

Plato believed that the world around us (trees, plants, factories, houses, footballs etc.) are mere illusions. They seem to exist but they are really shadows. The entire visible world is one huge trick.

Jim Tickner might take Plato to Milan, show him the San Siro stadium and exclaim: 'Look here, oh revered and mighty Greek one, this stadium is as crushingly real as a thumping Roy Keane reducer. Surely you don't believe it's an illusion?' Plato would sneer with intellectual disdain and address Tickner sharply

> You are an ignorant, unenlightened football nut. You spend your entire life chasing shadows. Get a life, Jim and contemplate real things like perfect triangles, squares and rectangles. Forget footballs and think about the perfect circle!

The Greek boffin was convinced that the real world is somehow invisible, unchanging and eternal. He insisted that human beings used to live in this heavenly and noble world before they were born. At birth our immortal souls fell from this splendid environment and became encased in the cement bag we call the human body. Plato was convinced that human beings are really prisoners living in the most appalling prison – the fleshly body. We are really immortal souls created to live in heaven but we have fallen from our true home. We think we belong to this place we call the earth but we are mistaken. We really belong *back home* in an invisible, ethereal and immaterial world. Plato urged his followers to shun the world and all its ephemeral pleasures and to embrace the lifestyle of the remote and austere philosopher. Plato contended that intellectuals and those who looked after their immortal souls would return to this heavenly bliss; the rest of us would be doomed to the horrors of reincarnation. In short we would become animals, insects and birds in the next cycle of rebirth.

We should stress at this juncture that Plato was a pagan and a heathen. He did not believe in the God of Abraham, Isaac and Jacob and yet his views on heaven and immortal souls have had an enormous influence on the Christian church. Plato understands salvation as snatching souls from an evil place (earth) and taking them to a much better place (heaven). Picture a woman who is sinking slowly into quicksand. We can easily imagine her screaming and yelling: 'Get me out of here. Is there anybody out there who can rescue me?' Picture now the handsome Indiana Jones riding out of the sunset and grinning as he saves the hot chick. He has rescued her and taken her out of her living nightmare. This is the platonic understanding of salvation.[10]

Those Christians who are influenced by the Great Greek Boffin are extremely numerous and they emphasise that the kingdom of God is really the kingdom of heaven. They urge us to prepare our immortal souls for its heavenly future. Such folk are convinced that watching, playing and thinking about football is a waste of time. Football can only damage your soul.

The kingdom of God refers to church and churchy activities

Howard did not enjoy his two years as a postman. Several large dogs in the Ruislip area did not appreciate the fragility of Howard's fingers as he deposited his many letters and parcels. One large Rottweiler took sadistic pleasure in growling and barking at the terrified former manager. And on one traumatic occasion a toothless and ageing Bloodhound covered him in saliva as he retreated from the door of a large and imposing mansion.

[10] We are indebted to Jon Baker for this illustration.

Such were the perils of postmanship. Bertha, his comely
and shapely wife, left him for a seventeen year old van
driver and Howard's house burned down when he neglected to turn off the gas and the chip pan exploded.

In these dark moments of despair and chagrin,
Howard began to pray. In the confines of his small and
dingy flat he began to call upon the name of the Lord.
Several days later he was walking along the road and
the minister from the local Anglican church approached
him. His opening gambit proceeded thus: 'Can I talk to
you for a few moments?' Howard was visibly stirred
and shaken. 'Has God spoken to you about my prayer-
ful entreaties?' 'No,' retorted the man of the cloth, 'I just
wanted to apologise to you about that wretched
Bloodhound that attacked you. Sherlock means no harm
but he does get a bit carried away sometimes.'

Howard accepted an invitation to the kindly minister's house and soon he had decided to give his life to the
Lord and joined one of the church's numerous house
groups. Before very long Howard had become a committed and enthusiastic member of St Swithin's Anglican
church. Despair and chagrin seemed but a distant memory now and Howard sat at the feet of the minister and
imbibed the great truths of the Christian faith. Things
were looking up for the former football manager.

Several months passed and one frosty winter morning, Howard received a phone call from the Gunners'
gaffer, Mr Arsene Wenger. 'Listen here,' waxed the
urbane Frenchman. 'I've heard all about your trials and
tribulations. I'm terribly sorry to hear about Bertha leav-
ing you and all that but I've got a proposal to put to you.
You've got an excellent eye for a good player, so why
don't you come and work at Arsenal as a football scout.
The money's not bad and you could do very well here.
What do you say?'

Howard was electrified by this wonderful opportunity and he promised the gaffer that he would get back to him within the week. Slightly nervously he approached his house group leader and asked his advice. Should he return to the world of football or would this be a tragic mistake? The house group leader frowned with displeasure and irritability. 'I can't believe that you are actually considering forsaking the Lord and returning to the world? Surely your church work and missionary activities must come first. Putting out the hymn books on Sunday is more important than watching football games.' Howard was disappointed with this firm advice but the very next day he telephoned Mr Wenger and turned down the job.

This parable about Howard and his decision to shun the world of football scouting can alert us to a particular understanding of the Christian faith. For many Christians today the kingdom of God is all about serving God in the church sphere of life. This perspective on the kingdom of God emphasises that the most important callings in the Christian life are those occupied by the minister, priest, vicar, curate or missionary.

These people are involved in *full-time* Christian ministry and their callings are perceived as superior to people who are otherwise engaged. Those who do not engage in these superior and more spiritual activities are not really involved in the kingdom of God. The average church punter is involved in kingdom activity only to the degree that they are involved in church work. For example an engineer or accountant would be praised if they were to assist the minister or priest by repairing the church roof or preparing meals for the church's outreach programme to homeless men and women.

Here, the minister is only interested in those members of the congregation who enjoy and contribute to ecclesiastical activity. Not everyone can become a minister or a priest but the laity can assist the spiritual elite by putting out the hymn books or visiting the old and the infirm. Those with musical and dramatic gifts can write hymns and craft sketches for church services. Those with business acumen and economic savvy can raise money for the church extension.

Sometimes this understanding of the kingdom can seem suspicious of football and those who are passionate about the game. More often, there is no overt hostility to the game – merely indifference and apathy. For many clergy today, football can elicit chuckles and titters but there is no sustained conviction that football can be redeemed or embraced by the kingdom of God. In this perspective, little is said to the congregation about their work and jobs. There are vague waftings about being nice, decent and moral but football like art, politics and scholarship is not nearly as important as church activity and involvement. It's OK to be involved in football as long as it does not interfere with church activity.

The kingdom of God is restricted to the future

A third understanding of the kingdom of God is sometimes referred to as the dispensationalist perspective. This view is very popular in the United States of America and our comments will be brief and to the point. On this view the kingdom of God has nothing to do with the present state of affairs. Indeed it has not arrived in any sense at all. We now live in a time of doom and gloom. The world is becoming more and more corrupt, twisted and perverted. Football, politics, economics, science and art etc. are inherently godless.

Suddenly like an unexpected goal from nowhere, God will rapture believers away from this evil age. This refers to a moment when all the righteous believers in Christ will suddenly vanish and join Christ in heaven. The wicked and unrighteous will be forced to endure a nightmare scenario on the earth. After a period of time the world will be completely destroyed and then God will create a brand new earth and Christ will reign with his people on this new earth. On this view the kingdom of God refers to this future reign of Christ. The kingdom of God has absolutely nothing to do with the present. This perspective has very little time or patience with those who love the game.

The kingdom of God is restricted to the present

Howard yawned as the church meeting drew to its close. The debate about the positioning of the new font had been passionate and exhausting. Mr Smythe had expressed considerable scepticism about the minister's intention to place the new font behind the crypt. 'Surely,' he grumbled, 'this would force Pat and Don Tuckerson to forsake their habitual seating arrangements and sit elsewhere.' Pat and Don concurred heartily with Mr Smythe and the minister seemed cantankerous as he explained yet again his precise reasons for the geographical repositioning.

Just then, as Howard yawned again, he was swept into a time tunnel by an invisible alien presence. He materialised in an Edwardian church in the year 1912. He was shocked and confused by this bizarre sequence of events. He noticed a newspaper skulking in a nearby pew and he picked it up and scanned its pages. There was no mention at all of Roy Keane, Ken Bates or Sir

Alex Ferguson on the back pages. There were several articles about a ship called the Titanic but hardly any reference to the beautiful game. Just then the minister approached and addressed Howard thus:

'We are desperate to find a person who will take on the church football team. Do you know of any person who might fit the bill?' Howard was surprised and excited to hear the game spoken of in such obviously glowing terms. 'Do you mean that you encourage involvement in football in your church?'

'Of course,' lisped the aristocratic curate 'Football, rugger and cricket are excellent team games and our working classes need the firm discipline and moral backbone that team sports can impart to that degenerate class. There's a war coming up, and we need proper men who will display unswerving loyalty and dedication to the cause. Christian men are becoming soft and spineless. Far too uppity and moaning about wages and factory conditions. Teach a man to play football properly and he will defend this Christian empire for the rest of his life. Blighty is in urgent peril and we need muscular Christians who can win the day.'

Just as the minister was finishing his eloquent homily, Howard was sucked into the time tunnel for the second time that day and he returned to the lively debate about fonts and crypts.

There are those who equate the kingdom of God with the British way of life or the American way of life. The emphasis here is upon present-day social movements and political aspirations. For example in Victorian and Edwardian England there were many Christians who enthused about the importance of team games to inculcate patriotism, respect for authority and firm discipline in young men. The idea behind this insisted that the playing fields of Eton and Harrow would prepare a new generation of decent fellows for service to the British Empire. Christian gentlemen would behave impeccably and properly in all circumstances; they would display the stiff-upper-lip and stoical courage of the British soldier; such chaps would be loyal citizens of the British Empire and the kingdom of God.

This perspective would contend that football can be a very positive and healthy form of activity if it promotes the proper British virtues. This view divinises or absolutises a particular nation or culture. This has happened in Britain, Germany and America. The focus here is not upon snatching souls to heaven or getting involved in church activities, it is contributing to any given society or culture. The very best of British, American or German culture is the kingdom of God. The focus here is upon the present and the future is not really mentioned.

We have now explored four popular but misleading views on the kingdom of God. We will now begin to examine the teaching of Jesus and present our alternative perspective.

6

The Kingdom of God brings God's Power into the World

If I were to ask you what the central theme of an Arnold Schwarzenegger film was, you wouldn't need to be a boffin like Plato to come up with the right answer! Have you ever studied the films *Commando*, *Total Recall*, *The Terminator*, *The Predator* and *Conan the Barbarian*? The typical Arnie film has a predictable plot. Somebody upsets the huge, muscular beefcake and the Austrian actor blows them away with Uzi submachine guns, grenades and rocket launchers. With supreme self-confidence the big guy *tools up* and defeats his numerous enemies. At the end of the film the man-mountain grins in triumph. Arnie may not be the world's most gifted conversationalist but he is just the kind of guy you need if evil villains are on the prowl in your neck of the woods.

What then is the central theme of the New Testament? Is it the journey of the immortal soul as it floats heavenward? Or the urgent obligation to replace the church organ? Perhaps the teaching of Jesus is urging us to forsake the evil world and live on a pillar for thirty years.

The central theme of the New Testament is the coming of the kingdom of God. The Greek word for this crunch theme is *basileia* and this term appears about a hundred times in the teaching of Jesus. In the gospel of Mark the very first thing Jesus says is this

'The time has come,' he said. 'The kingdom of God is near. Repent and believe the good news!'

Mark 1:15

When we hear about good news we are often excited and cheerful. Suppose you are a fan of Bristol Rovers (like Jim) and in a Monty Python parallel universe your team wins the European Cup; you would be over the moon and extremely chuffed. You would embrace strangers, dance a jig and cackle with laughter. Abandoned to joy and merriment you would telephone all your pals and relive those magic moments.

When Jesus spoke about the coming of the kingdom he was similarly excited and exultant. He was declaring that something truly wonderful was just about to happen.

Comical football vignette

Richard had been the perfect chairman. He had lavished his care and wealth upon Fulchester United. For ten long years the team had enjoyed victory after victory. They had accrued seven premiership titles, three European Cup triumphs, two UEFA Cup successes and six FA Cup wins. The players were happy with their modest salaries and supported numerous charities with unfailing vigour. Happiness and bonhomie pervaded the club; the fans were treated like old friends and the tea-ladies revelled in the care and concern that was dispensed to them by the busy staff. And then one day Richard contracted a mysterious illness that knocked him out like a Mike Tyson uppercut. For several months he languished in hospital; his breathing was heavy and laboured; his fevered brow was hot and clammy. And then one dark winter night he called to Karen, the beautiful and attentive nurse, and croaked: 'I am too ill to continue as chairman of Fulchester United, tell the vice-chairman, John, that he must now take my place.' And then Richard sank into a deep and mysterious coma.

Evil John licked his lips. 'I am to be boss now!' he whispered triumphantly. And so John worked his evil and insidious magic. He brought in an incompetent and visionless manager, and together they brewed poison and skulduggery in the boot-room. Before long the best players were begging for transfers and mediocre journeymen were purchased from third division outfits. The club began to crumble and wither as John's stewardship of the club became increasingly pugnacious and destructive. In the glory days, Fulchester's finest had controlled the ball with instant and effortless skill; now the ball would hit a player's chest and hurtle like a rocket into the adjacent car park.

John treated all his employees with disdain and contempt. The tea-ladies were rebuked and chided as they delivered their trays of tea and chocolate biscuits. The groundsmen were insulted on a daily basis and young players were bullied and humiliated by the senior professionals. The young pups were terrified as John prowled about the club premises spraying vitriol and grabbing tender ears with sharp fingers. Fear and loathing lurked in every corner.

The fans became increasingly violent and shameless. They chanted obscene songs and dressed up in gorilla costumes as they hurled racist slogans at black players. Their ring-leaders were cruel and loathsome yobs who whispered venomous lies into the ears of their young offspring. Many supporters would bring crates of lager beer and hurl the empty bottles at opposing fans. Drunken cackles, burps and belches were omnipresent. John watched on from his penthouse suite and smiled with deep and lasting satisfaction. 'I wonder what Richard would think if he could see what I have done to his beloved Fulchester United!'

Just then the telephone rang and John picked up the receiver. It was Karen, the devoted nurse. She cried, 'Richard has woken up, John. He's just getting dressed and he's coming back.' John's smiling demeanour vanished in the twinkling of an eye as his face twitched and convulsed with fear and dread. Richard was coming back!

Mr Zebub is as sick as a parrot

This parable can help us to understand the dramatic moment in the gospel when Jesus announced the coming of the kingdom of God. As with any analogy you can press the comparison too far and end up in the quagmires of total nonsense. Of course I am not suggesting that the Almighty slipped into a coma but the significant point should be clear enough.

It is not fashionable to talk about the devil in our modern times. Indeed for many, reference to this shadowy figure activates discomfort and displeasure. But how can you talk about football if you ignore the opposing team? Football doesn't make any sense if you ignore the clash of teams, the battle of the Titans. Sir Alex Ferguson bristles with rage as his great opponent Arsene

Wenger insinuates critical and demeaning theories about Manchester United. There is and always will be dramatic contests in the game that cry out for fulfilment! Will Real Madrid destroy all their opponents and win the European Cup for the tenth time? Will Bristol Rovers avoid relegation to the Nationwide Conference League? This is the very essence of the game, its glory and its madness. Can we imagine a cup competition where only one team contests for the silverware? Could we imagine a league with only one team? 'Absurd,' I hear you cry.

Just as Captain Hook confronts his great and worthy opponent Peter Pan so Jesus confronts his great and not so worthy opponent – the devil. Lucifer, Satan, the prince of this world, call him what you will, has stolen the world from God and turned it into his kingdom of darkness. Just as John ruins and ravages Fulchester United, so the devil ruins and ravages God's club – the world.

In the gospel of Luke we are told that this great opponent of God lays claim to the entire world and declares: 'This belongs to me. I can do what I like with this huge spherical object.' Listen to Luke as he exposes the serpent's tactical strategies:

> The devil led him up to a high place and showed him in an instant all the kingdoms of the world. And he said to him, 'I will give you all their authority and splendour, for it has been given to me, and I can give it to anyone I want to. So if you worship me, it will all be yours.' Jesus answered, 'It is written: "Worship the Lord your God and serve him only."'
>
> Luke 4:5–8

Satan lays claim to God's world. The evil guvnor controls and dominates life on this planet. He can be compared to the Mafia. He is the supreme Godfather! Years ago I taught English as a foreign language to a wonderful bunch of Italian students. One of the girls was called Francesca and she came from Reggio Calabria in the deep south of Italy. She told me a story about the Mafia that will help to illustrate my point. She and her family had arrived at their country villa only to discover that the water had been turned off. They contacted a local plumber and he duly arrived. But nothing could be done. Francesca's family telephoned the local council who explained that the local Mafia was demanding a bribe. The family refused to play ball and for several weeks the taps refused to co-operate. Finally they could stand the discomfort no more and they paid up. The very next day the taps gushed with water. This part of Italy is still heavily under Mafia domination but as you walk along the streets in Reggio Calabria you would not notice it; however, scratch the surface and you will encounter this malign and corrupting force. From a tactical point of view the devil and the Mafia play the same kind of game. Not for them the crude and unsophisticated 442 formation; with the Mafia and the devil you do not even suspect that they are playing.

Tragic football vignette

We have already explored in chapter 2 how the kingdom of darkness has perverted the beautiful game. One of the most striking manifestations of evil pervading football took place in the former Yugoslavia under the stewardship of one Zeijko Raznatovic.

The career of Mr Raznatovic, otherwise known as Arkan, has embraced juvenile delinquency, bank robbery, professional assassination, paramilitary soldiery,

torture of ethnic minorities and chairmanship of a leading football club.

Mr Raznatovic's reign as president of Obilic Belgrade
was one of the most sordid chapters in the history of
European football. He brought some success to
Belgrade's third club but his methods were brutal and
corrupt. In particular Arkan employed paramilitary
mercenaries (dubbed the Tigers) to intimidate and beat
up opposing players who played too well or scored
goals against Obilic Belgrade! There is also evidence that
he filled opposition changing rooms with sleeping gas
so as to make their players drowsy and lethargic.
Perhaps it is not unsurprising that Mr Raznatovic was
shot dead in the lobby of Belgrade's Intercontinental
Hotel on 15 January 2000. We could say that Lucifer
rules and reigns by employing Arkan and others like
him to do his bidding.[11]

Now that we have some cursory insight into the
career and tactical leanings of Mr B.L. Zebub we can
acquaint ourselves with the Supreme Gaffer's tactical
response to the father of lies. In the gospel we encounter
Jesus confronting the devil and throwing down the
gauntlet. Here is a typical passage

> They went to Capernaum, and when the Sabbath came,
> Jesus went into the synagogue and began to teach. The
> people were amazed at his teaching, because he taught
> them as one who had authority, not as the teachers of the
> law. Just then a man in their synagogue who was pos-
> sessed by an evil spirit cried out, 'What do you want
> with us, Jesus of Nazareth? Have you come to destroy
> us? I know who you are – the Holy One of God!' 'Be

---

[11] We are indebted to the October 2002 edition of the sports
magazine *Four Four Two* for information about Arkan.

quiet!' said Jesus sternly. 'Come out of him!' The evil
spirit shook the man violently and came out of him with
a shriek.

Mark 1:21–26

We can easily imagine Mr Zebub writhing and wincing
in pain as his miserable journeymen are dispatched with
casual aplomb. I remember so vividly when Maradona
was playing for Naples in Serie A. He was sitting on the
bench nursing a slight groin strain and his team was los-
ing by three goals to nil against Roma. The team from
the capital city seemed smug and supremely confident
of victory. And then in the sixtieth minute the
Argentinian wizard came on as a substitute and
the game turned almost instantaneously. He bossed the
game, driving his team forward; his power running and
pinpoint passing created havoc in the Roma defence. He
ran through the opposition, riding hospital tackles and
scoring goals with consummate mastery. The Roma
defenders looked absolutely terrified and helpless as the
master ran them ragged and brought victory to his team.
I have never witnessed one player terrorise and bludg-
eon an opposing team in such extraordinary fashion.
This one incident is my Ace of Spades when I confront
Tickner with my sustained thesis that Maradona is the
greatest player of all time. Tickner can only murmur
'enough' as he buries his head in his hands, crestfallen
and outgunned by my imperious arguments.

We could say that Christ came into the world to
invade the kingdom of darkness. He confronts the devil
and rebukes him. He elicits fear and dread in his great
opponent as he penetrates into the territory of the prince
of darkness and mows down the hostile powers which
have blighted the world. Not only does Christ tackle and
outplay B.L. Zebub, he comes to restore and heal the

subjects of his kingdom who have been damaged and hurt by the fall we discussed in chapter 2. In the gospel of Luke we are told the following story about a woman who was very distressed

> On a Sabbath Jesus was teaching in one of the synagogues, and a woman was there who had been crippled by a spirit for eighteen years. She was bent over and could not straighten up at all. When Jesus saw her, he called her forward and said to her, 'Woman, you are set free from your infirmity.' Then he put his hands on her, and immediately she straightened up and praised God.
>
> Luke 13:10–13

When Jesus comes onto the park, this is the kind of thing that happens. Blind people begin to see. Deaf people start to hear. Lame people begin to walk. Paralysed people stand up and dead people come alive. All of these miracles signal defeat and termination of contract to Mr Zebub and his repulsive henchmen. The devil enslaves the world in his vice-like grip and Christ comes to bring shalom to his wonderful but broken world. All of the miracles of Christ (with the one exception of the cursing of the fig tree) are miracles of restoration – restoration to health, restoration to life, restoration to freedom from demonic possession.

Comical football vignette

To what can we compare the kingdom of God? Once upon a time there was a beautiful city in the south of France. Happy French people laughed and chortled as they cavorted in the warm sunshine. Public feasts were popular and embraced at least fourteen different courses with appropriate vintage wines to complement the refined and sophisticated cuisine. Frog's legs, snails, *foie gras*, steak *au poivre* and *lapin à la moutarde* were common fare; there was not a porkpie to be seen in any shop or restaurant. Children discussed complex novels by Emile Zola and Gustave Flaubert and the mature adults displayed their mastery of difficult philosophical masterpieces by Descartes and Jean-Paul Sartre. Irony, wit and *savoir vivre* ruled the roost; even the beggars were droll, articulate and cultured.

A football tournament had been organised by the merchants of that fair city. The mayor had written to the English king and inquired if his majesty would condescend to send over a football team and enter the tourney. The English king was pleased to receive this invitation. Thousands of young English yeomen accompanied the team and set off on their long journey to that distant land.

As soon as the English arrived in that town, they decided to visit the local inns, restaurants and cafes. It did not take long for the impact of alcohol to prevail. Cries of 'wallop' filled the air as drunken fans broke wind and belched with alarming regularity. Spitting and swearing became fashionable and the local people became uneasy and alarmed. By the third evening of their stay, supporters of Millwall were vomiting on the restaurant tables and leering drunkenly at the local girls. Fights began to break out and boorish yobs displayed their flick-knives in the streets and boulevards of that unhappy town. Before long the drunken foreigners were organising dog fights and badger baiting amusements. The local French folk recoiled in horror and retreated to their homes where they were able to read the poets Baudelaire, Verlaine and Rimbaud without the intrusion of raucous, vulgar laughter. On the fourth day the hooligans invaded the flats and houses of those cultured and urbane intellectuals and every nook and cranny of that sorry town became defiled by the English presence.

Finally in their darkest hour the local people decided to contact the police and inform them of the English invasion. The French police force arrived promptly and, aided by their water cannons and tear gas, attacked the drunken yobbos with firm and forceful vigour. The English hooligans were routed and defeated in a matter of hours and were dragged into the surrounding countryside and imprisoned in large French barns. At last the town was free and spontaneous singing, dancing and feasting commenced with considerable intensity. At last the loathsome enemy had been defeated.

7

The Kingdom of God is Here but not Fully Here

Five football supporters were walking along the road one day. The sun was shining brightly and the grass seemed so lush and green. The sky was cloudless and bright blue. Gentle, docile cows were chewing the cud in nearby fields and the tulips looked radiant as they fluttered gently in the breeze. It was a glorious day and the prospect of the big match against Watford was immensely appealing.

Phillip had belonged to F-Troop for as long as he could remember. He was an affluent and articulate barrister, married to a beautiful upper class girl and proud father of two bouncing babies but he loved a feisty punch-up and knew how to organise a good rumble. The lads started to sing. 'Millwall, Millwall. No one likes us. We don't care.' Their voices blended splendidly.

Just then an Asian lad came into view and the lads winked at each other knowingly. 'Bundle' they bellowed as they launched into action. Ten minutes later the Asian boy was lying unconscious and blood was splattered all over his white shirt. The laughing lads raced away at top speed but a police car appeared as if from nowhere and the barrister and his chums were nicked by the Old Bill. Phillip was tried for Grievous Bodily Harm and went down for seven years. His wife Penelope left him and married a solicitor who preferred the game of Scrabble to the game of football.

Brian and the kingdom of God

Just like Phillip, Jesus has also committed assault and battery! Listen to Matthew as he alludes to this shocking and violent case

> Then they brought him a demon-possessed man who was blind and mute, and Jesus healed him, so that he could both talk and see. All the people were astonished and said, 'Could this be the Son of David?' But when the Pharisees heard this, they said, 'It is only by Beelzebub, the prince of demons, that this fellow drives out demons.' Jesus knew their thoughts and said to them, 'Every kingdom divided against itself will be ruined, and every city or household divided against itself will not stand. If Satan drives out Satan, he is divided against himself. How then can his kingdom stand? And if I drive out demons by Beelzebub, by whom do your people drive them out? So then, they will be your judges. But if I drive out demons by the Spirit of God, then the kingdom of God has come upon you. Or again, how can anyone enter a strong man's house and carry off his possessions unless he first ties up the strong man? Then he can rob his house.'
>
> Matthew 12:22–29

If this had gone to court, the police would have had an open and shut case. Jesus has healed and restored a blind man who couldn't speak. Imagine this lad's intense frustration and longing. This bloke was unable to play football, watch football and talk football. Locked inside a world of darkness and despair, he couldn't luxuriate in this colourful and multi-faceted theatre of dreams – God's creation. And then he is assaulted by the kingdom of God. The healing shalom of Yahweh breaks into his darkness and loneliness and he can see and he can talk. If he had lived today he could have spent many happy hours watching and re-watching that goal by Maradona that has been voted the finest ever. (And if you have never seen that goal then you shouldn't be reading this book! You should be reading a novel by Jilly Cooper or a play by Anton Chekhov.)

When I meet this man at the resurrection (more on this later) I am going to ask him some pretty pointed questions about his first experience of the kingdom of God. What was the first thing/person he saw? Was he completely stunned by the brightness of the sun? And what were his first words? I'm particularly interested in the reaction of his nearest and dearest. What did his mum say? I bet they had an interesting and enjoyable chat. Did he open a bottle of pomagne or whatever festive beverage was available? Did he encounter Jesus at any other moment in his life? I'm really looking forward to finding out. When we've got all this cleared up I shall definitely introduce Brian (that's what I think he was probably called) to Tickner. We shall then engage in a thoughtful and lively theological debate. We shall probe him on first century Jewish leisure activities and find out if Brian had any hobbies. He might have explored this possibility during the remainder of his life as a sighted, talking person. We might conclude that hobbies presuppose a certain amount of leisure time that was not available to first century Jews. We'll find out one day!

Without doubt Tickner and I will expound our understanding of the cultural mandate (discussed earlier) and explain how human beings have developed and unfolded sport and in particular the beautiful game during the past two thousand years. We hope he will share our enthusiasm. When we've had our fill of laughing and conversing we might even ask him if he would like to join us for a game. Jim will help Brian to control the ball and I will show him my famous drag-back. It should be a lot of fun. Tickner will warn Brian that if one of the seraphs is playing in goal it will be almost impossible to score any goals. That's always been the problem with those very big angels; let's be quite open and frank about this. They only get one mention in the Bible (Is. 6) and they can sometimes seem rather stern and forbidding.

Assault and battery

This passage is not only important because it refers to our future mate Brian but it makes it abundantly clear that the kingdom of God has already arrived! When Jesus healed people and drove out evil spirits, the kingdom of God was breaking into the present. It wasn't just some vague future hope – heaven or whatever you might call it. This kingdom thing has been invading us for two thousand plus years. What a scorcher!

It's also helpful to point out that Jesus has broken into the devil's house, tied him up and nicked his possessions. The boy Luke adds that Jesus has stolen the devil's armour and left him almost naked wearing only his underpants and socks (Lk. 11:22). Sometimes when I'm struggling with the house work and the care of young children I like to remind myself of these magnificent assault and battery episodes in the life and ministry of our saviour. Perceptive theologians have pointed out that Mr Zebub is now bound with a rope that can be lengthened or shortened!

Jewish understanding of the kingdom of God

We now need to explore the kind of kingdom that Brian and his mum and dad were probably expecting. Many people are aware that the land of Israel at the time of Jesus was occupied by an invading Roman army. The country was full of social unrest and political agitation. Terrorist groups were fermenting rebellion and revolution. To say that there was tension in the air would be an understatement! Most Jewish punters were convinced that God would send a powerful warrior who would raise an army and drive the Romans out. This man would be a bit like an Arnold Schwarzenegger character in that he would tool up, recruit some tough and determined soldiers and organise a massive bundle. The Jewish firm would take on the Roman firm and God's anointed servant would be crowned as king.

We could say that the Jews expected the kingdom of God to come suddenly and all at once. It's a bit like a single FA Cup round where you sort out the opposing team in one single dramatic encounter. At three o'clock Fulham are still in the cup and then at five o'clock they've been dumped out by Liverpool. One moment the Fulham boys are in the cup and then bang – Michael Owen pulls the trigger and they're dead. Done and dusted. That's the FA Cup and that's what Brian thought would happen when the kingdom of God finally comes. Messiah turns up. Messiah tools up. Messiah fights with pals. Messiah is crowned king. Romans go home.

Everybody has a big party. The kingdom of God has finally arrived! Even my son Emile can grasp this kind of show-down.

Comical football vignette

The peculiar and distinctive teaching of Jesus about the kingdom is rather more complicated and subtle than this FA Cup scenario. It's more like a two leg tie à la UEFA Cup or final stages of the Champions League. Do you remember the crunch two leg semi-final tie between Manchester United and Juventus in 1999? I watched both games with Tickner.

Anyway let me talk you through those two fine games. For the first leg Jim and I were in agony as Juventus pummelled United with their flair and power running. Edgar Davids and Zinedine Zidane were outstanding and the Manchester boys looked outgunned and outclassed. In the final seconds of the game Ryan Giggs scored a desperately needed goal and the score settled at 1-1. To be totally honest neither of us supports Manchester United but we do like it when our boys do well in Europe. We were relieved but pessimistic about the match in Turin. Juventus looked a very classy outfit!

Loads of things happened in those two weeks between the home tie and the glory moments over in Turin. Tickner passed his driving test on the seventh attempt and managed to get a job as a book-seller in Waterstones. I crashed our yellow Fiesta and took my daughter Hannah to her first school disco. Jim's wife Lou hurled herself into their new garden and quite literally transformed it from a desert into an oasis and my wife Anne cleared out the garden shed. Many things transpired in those two weeks.

Jim and I turned on the telly with some trepidation and foreboding as the second leg kicked off in Turin. During the first eleven minutes Filippo Inzaghi managed to score two goals for the Italian outfit and to add insult to injury Jim had failed to produce any reasonable snacks for the big game. Brooding and pensive, our conversations became muted and monosyllabic as the prospect of a European Cup triumph seemed increasingly remote and implausible. And then the game turned. Roy Keane got his head to a Beckham corner and the ball rifled into the back of the net. We gasped with pleasure and surprise. Another sublime header by Yorke brought an equaliser before half-time and all of us could sniff faint waftings of glory as Tim Bowman was shown the door and dispatched to purchase baked goods at half-time. In the second half there was some desperate defending from the Manchester boys and then Dwight Yorke slipped through the Juventus defence and was hauled to the ground by the goalkeeper but the ball was picked up by Andy Cole and he slotted it home cool as the proverbial cucumber. Manchester United had defeated that superb Juventus team and we couldn't believe it! Oh the sweetness of unexpected victory!

Why all this inane and trite football talk? This football vignette can help us to understand Jesus' unique perspective on the coming of the kingdom. Firstly he announces the arrival of the kingdom which corresponds to the first leg (Jesus' first coming). Then the kingdom manifests itself in this present sin-stained age in an unexpected and hidden way which corresponds to the two week interval. Finally God delivers the decisive blow to all evil and Mr Zebub in the second leg (Jesus' second coming). We could say that now in this present evil age we only catch glimpses of the kingdom of God. It's here but not fully here.

When we speak about glimpsing the kingdom of God now, we are straying into difficult and challenging terrain. It's almost as if we've wandered into the dressing room and Terry Venables is delivering a complex and obscure lecture on the merits of his famous diamond tactical formation. The players don't understand what El Tel is talking about and neither do we. That's how hard this topic is. Very tricky and elusive.

Bristol Church League

Fortunately Jim has been able to furnish us with the perfect illustration of this challenging and mysterious aspect of the topic in hand. Jim is the proud captain of the Bristol Sanctuary 11 and his team plays in the Bristol Church League. A few days ago I went round to see Jim and he was in sad and sombre mood. Sensitive as ever I quickly noticed his gloomy and cheerless demeanour and probed him about the cause of his chagrin. Jim explained to me that he had just played in the worst game of his life! The lads had been playing a team from the Bristol Suburban fifth division in the first round of the Gloucester FA Primary Cup. The first ten minutes of the game had been encouraging for Jim and the boys; they were all over the opposition like a cheap suit and victory for the Sanctuary 11 seemed a foregone conclusion.

Suddenly the atmosphere changed as Sanctuary's top striker was hacked down in the box and the referee waved the game on. The opposition had sniffed the stale odour of defeat and they had decided to intimidate the referee and kick lumps out of the Sanctuary team. Jim was aggrieved and alerted the referee to the sin-stained attitude of the opposing team. His urgent entreaties were spurned as the referee booked Jim and continued stubbornly in his errant and foolhardy ways. Jim was elbowed in the face on two separate occasions and other members of the team were punched and kicked. Not only this but Sanctuary's valiant and stalwart supporter Tracy Tickner (Jim's sister-in-law) was reviled and abused by the supporters of the opposing team. Tracy, Jim and all the other Sanctuary players felt defiled and sickened by this brutal affair. Some of the most unpleasant features of the fall had conspired to ruin that day.

What a stunning contrast to a normal game in the Bristol Church League! When teams play in that league there is always a word of prayer before the game begins. Jim's favourite football prayer goes something like this

> We know that God loves the game and we pray that you will bless us as we play open, honest and attractive football. We ask that no one will be hurt or injured. We ask this in Jesus' name.

Curiously enough all the players, Christian and non-Christian, are very respectful of this God-honouring moment. Games are characterised by good humour, kindness and fair play. On several occasions players have refused to take penalties and have gently suggested to the ref that no foul had been committed. Sometimes the penalty taker will pass the ball to the goalkeeper if he is convinced that the penalty was not deserved! Players are normally completely honest about corners, throw-ins and free kicks. Some referees have told Jim how much they enjoy officiating in this league and rejoice at the absence of intimidation, reducers and blatant cheating. One non-Christian player, Roy, has been struck by the different spirit that infuses the football in the Bristol Church League. Players are not as a rule scythed down while others gob, moan and swear. Of course there are silly lunges and the odd expletive but the general tone of the league is the total opposite to many of the barbaric games that disgrace the parks and fields of this green and pleasant land.

There is also a delightful and cheeky banter that percolates through the Bristol Church League. Players enjoy joshing and joking as they explore God's creation with speed, movement, pirouettes, shimmies, dummies, chest-traps and explosive thumpings of the leather ball. Cruel, mocking humour is not welcome in this league. The players love a laugh and wild cackles can often be heard as they play the beautiful game but the teasing is gentle, good-humoured and gracious. We could say that there are glimpses of the merciful and tender rule of God in this league. The kingdom of God has not arrived in its total fullness but it's still there – hidden and mysterious.

There are much more public and obvious manifestations of the kingdom of God in football. Recall for a moment the World Cup final of 2002. At the very end of the game three Brazilian players removed their famous yellow shirts to reveal undershirts which declared – JESUS LOVES ME and I BELONG TO JESUS. Not only this; the entire Brazilian team and support staff knelt in obvious praise and gratitude to the Supreme Gaffer. It was almost as if they were saying: 'Dear God, we've won the World Cup and we're over the moon! Thank you for making this game and we hope you enjoyed our silky skills! Amen!' The BBC commentator John Motson did not deign to comment on this obvious act of worship. Gary Lineker, Alan Hanson, Ian Wright and Martin O'Neill also seemed bemused and discomforted by this Brazilian act of worship. At times even the cold, secular contempt of the BBC can be flustered and shaken by

God's hidden and unexpected invasion of this game we know and love.

8

The Kingdom of God Embraces All of Life

The Reverend Cedric Puddles was composed and alert as he stepped forward to deliver his Sunday sermon. He had a challenging message for his flock and he wasn't going to hold back. Now was the moment to stand up and be counted. He began to address his congregation thus:

'I have been an ordained Anglican vicar for some thirty years and as I approach my retirement, I look back on my life with both pleasure and regret. A life of service to one's flock is never easy. As a young curate, working in the East End of London, I can remember a wonderful moment that will remain forever etched upon my now fading memory. I recall entering the church on a cold and frosty morning; the pews beckoned me in all their glory and I saw at the end of the church two young toddlers playing by the font. Young Smithy and his brother Algy.

'And I thought to myself: "Isn't this what the gospel is all about? Smithy and Algy playing by the font." And at that moment Mrs Smythe-Robinson was carefully laying out the hymn books; her face beaming with joy and pride.

'And Mrs Kempton-Smythe, valiant and outspoken member of the PCC, was dusting the font, her hair shining with a heavenly glory. And again I mused: "Isn't this what our faith is all about?" I felt as if the Lord, himself, had snatched me up into glory, like Enoch. And Enoch walked with God; and he was not for God took him.

'And there by the church door stood our virtuous and most honest verger Mr Pickling-Smythe, polishing the door handle. And I thought to myself: "Isn't this what our creed boldly declares?"

'And then I heard the voices of some young unruly teenagers, football lager louts, as they are called in the tabloid newspapers, returning from their all-night revelries. Drunken voices and drunken songs. Let me tell you what they were singing: *"They fly so high, they reach the sky and then like Tottenham they fade and die. Tottenham always running, Arsenal running too. We're for ever blowing bubbles, pretty bubbles in the sky."*

'The hideous hiss of the lower orders bellowing out their football incantations reminded me of the pagan Canaanite fertility rites. The stench of the great unwashed flooded through my nostrils and my church. Ah the soothing and oh so ephemeral glimpse of heavenly bliss vanished in a puff of pagan smoke.

'And I thought to myself: "I know where I am going. Yes I have my assurance of eternal life, my ticket to heavenly glory." Oh the glories of heaven. Heavenly fonts, heavenly crypts, heavenly pews and a glistening heavenly spire. And Jesus sitting serenely at the heavenly organ. Isn't that what our Lord taught us?

'One day we will all be in that heavenly church together singing hymn after hymn. Our worship, our heavenly worship will know no end. Quiet times, gentle acts of sharing, flicking joyfully through the Psalter Hymnal. Of that there will be no end.

'But the concupiscent carousing and the idle frolicking of our earthly life will be no more. The sordid, salacious carnal pleasures, the gambling, the imbibing of wicked juices, the putrid and fetid gossiping of the worldly will be no more. The dank, dark deeds of leering, loathsome West Ham supporters and the lustful world of sex-crazed teenagers will be but a distant memory.

'I remember that sublime moment, those two toddlers, Smithy and Algy playing by the font. And I thought to myself: "Isn't this what Christianity is all about?"'

Different spheres of life

This spoof on the sermon of an Anglican vicar is not as far-fetched as it might sound. I have heard many sermons in this genre. Somehow for Cedric Puddles significant, important life has been sucked into the vortex of the church sphere. Puddles is besotted with ecclesiastical life and he is convinced that life in the *church* is superior to life in the *world*. For many people today God is equated with fonts, spires, steeples, organs, choirs, funerals, vicars, vergers, priests, nuns, missionaries, monasteries, jumble sales, cassocks, dog collars, stained glass windows and collection plates. These people and things belong to the ecclesiastical sphere of life.

When we read the New Testament, we encounter a very different picture of life and God. God is not portrayed as some old, earnest and eccentric buffer who wears unfashionable and dowdy clothing. God has little if anything to do with fonts and spires. God is the great

King who comes to bring his royal rule of justice, peace and mercy to his broken and sin-stained world. Let's briefly examine a passage in the book of Acts which will help us to expose the ugly perversions of Puddles and his ilk.

> They devoted themselves to the apostles' teaching and to the fellowship, to the breaking of bread and to prayer. Everyone was filled with awe, and many wonders and miraculous signs were done by the apostles. All the believers were together and had everything in common. Selling their possessions and goods, they gave to anyone as he had need. Every day they continued to meet together in the temple courts. They broke bread in their homes and ate together with glad and sincere hearts, praising God and enjoying the favour of all the people. And the Lord added to their number daily those who were being saved.
>
> Acts 2:42–47

In this attractive and exciting scenario we can distinguish different spheres of life that are being redeemed and transformed by God. For example the buying and selling of possessions and goods has been radically assaulted by the kingdom of God! Do you remember our fanciful vignette of Ronaldo and Roberto Carlos in chapter 3? We could say that economic life is being invaded by the rule of God. Instead of rich, selfish footballers accumulating seven or eight Ferraris, our Brazilian ball-merchants are investing their time and money in the kingdom of God. And that's exactly what was going on in the infant Christian community. The wisdom enshrined in the Jubilee and Sabbath laws was breaking out in new and dynamic ways.

The passage also refers to our homes and families. This sphere of life is also crying out for the kingdom of God. We can imagine mums, dads, toddlers, babies, grandmothers and grandfathers loving each other, playing together and celebrating – singing, making toast, frying eggs and watching sausages sizzle and spit. Doing the whole thing to the glory of God. This sphere of life is being invaded by the kingdom of God. Oh and yes they do go to the temple, worship and listen to the teaching of the apostles but this is only a small part of the total game! Going to church is just one small slice of the action.

Puddles is hideously misled and deceived in his understanding of the gospel. He's a bit like the manager who only likes centre-halves and insists that every player in his team should be a stopper. I have the greatest respect for Sol Campbell but a team of Sol Campbells would be as impoverished as a team of Ryan Giggses.

God delights in all of life. Our God loves painting, poetry, science, sport, business, education, families, comedy; the list goes on and on. Our God doesn't want us to suck all these good things into a church and suffocate them to death with ecclesiastical smog and fog. To do this does not bring honour to God.

Oppressive institutions

It isn't only the church institution which can play bully and pervert life! Businesses and football clubs can be just as oppressive and all-consuming as churches. There are companies that quite literally drive their employees to an early death. In Japan, for example, there is a medical condition that refers to people who die early because they have worked too hard for their employers!

There are men and women who work hundreds of hours every week for their companies and spend almost no time with their spouses and children. There is the sad story of a Japanese woman who can only speak to her husband by e-mail because he is never at home to talk to. He quite literally lives in his office (bed and toothbrush in a cupboard) and has no time for his family. He is driven to do this by the workaholic expectations of his employers. We could say that this man has had his life sucked into the cruel vortex of business life. This kind of oppressive business is not restricted to Japan; it happens frequently in Britain. I have a friend who regularly works until two o'clock in the morning; his life is dehumanised by the frantic and never-ending demands of his job. At the end of the day his employers don't give two figs about his exhaustion and impoverished family life; they merely mumble mantras like loyalty and commitment.

As I have said, football clubs can be just as all-consuming and oppressive. We have already been alerted to the pagan and idolatrous perspective of Bill Shankly in chapter 1. There are numerous stories of Shankly's obsession with the game which illustrate how football clubs can run roughshod over their employees. Shanks would never speak to players who had injuries. He would only speak to them through a third party! Somehow an injured player had quite literally ceased to exist! Shankly viewed his players as mere appendages who belonged body and soul to Liverpool Football Club. He even remarked on one occasion that players who did not try hard enough to win a game should be sent to prison!

In the excellent book *Football Confidential* Ian Bent writes of a conversation between the tough defender Tommy Smith and the legendary Liverpool gaffer.

Smith to Shankly: 'My thigh is still a bit sore, but I think I could play if I wore a bandage.'

Shankly to Fagan: 'Tell him, Joe. He has got no chance of playing.'

Fagan to Smith: 'The boss says you have no chance of playing if you wear a bandage.'

Smith to Fagan: 'Tell him to *** off. It is not his leg, it's mine.'

Shankly to Smith: (breaking his golden rule of never speaking to an injured player) 'Oh, no, son. You are wrong, son. It is not your leg. It is Liverpool Football Club's leg.'[12]

Stories of managers who spend every waking moment consumed by the game are legion. There are many children and spouses of football addicts who are the victims of football idolatry. These people have been sucked often willingly into the vortex of football. They are not normally preoccupied by money; they just give every ounce of their talent and energy to the game. Tragically this managerial mindset can take on young players at a tender and vulnerable age and later discard them like so much flotsam and jetsam when their legs, ankles and thighs no longer suit the club. Young lads can often leave the game bitter, disillusioned and jaded. The vicious vortex of football idolatry has left them uneducated, inarticulate and unable to cope with modern life.

We have all met bullies in our lives. Jim made the unfortunate mistake of growing up in a rough neighbourhood of Bristol. He has told me that he was often

---

[12] Ian Bent, *Football Confidential*, 59 (the *** are mine!).

bullied and intimidated by beefy, tattooed heathens who would beat him into a pulsating purée of skin and blood. Fortunately I was born into a respectable and educated middle class social milieu and the worst bullying I experienced was chums chortling when I was unable to locate my trunks for the afternoon swimming lesson.

I introduce this jocular and buffoonish reference to bullying in order to ram home a central insight. Institutions can bully and destroy peoples' lives. Churches can do this. Football clubs can do this. Business companies can do this. Schools can do this. Even families can become bullies and tyrants. Consider the film *The Godfather*. When Don Corleone mumbles and croaks in his inarticulate and laconic fashion we encounter yet another idolatry. His family has become a false god and all must bow down and worship. Or else! Upset the Don and you will wake up to find your prize-winning stallion's bloodied head beside you. Nice.

This is the way modern secular people live! They don't bow down and worship rats, crocodiles and frogs. They bow down and worship institutions. They say to football – be my god. They say to economic institutions – I'll worship you. They say to their families – you are everything! When we study the Bible we become aware that all human institutions have important but limited callings. This is how the boy Micah made this point three thousand years ago.

> But as for me, I am filled with power, with the Spirit of the Lord, and with justice and might, to declare to Jacob his transgression, to Israel his sin. Hear this, you leaders of the house of Jacob, you rulers of the house of Israel, who despise justice and distort all that is right; who build Zion with bloodshed, and Jerusalem with wickedness.

> Her leaders judge for a bribe, her priests teach for a price,
> and her prophets tell fortunes for money.
>
> Micah 3:8–11a

Just as in our passage from the book of Acts we can distinguish different spheres of life. The prophet is lambasting
rulers, judges, priests and prophets who have betrayed
their callings. We could say that he is addressing the leading institutions of his day and rebuking them in much the
same way that Alex Ferguson might deliver a stinging
tirade against journalists and the media. In effect the lad
Micah is calling these institutions to be faithful to what the
Supreme Gaffer wanted them to do in the first place. Rulers
are supposed to maintain justice and make just laws.
Judges are meant to punish guilty people fairly and acquit
the innocent. Priests have the task of teaching people God's
law. Prophets are supposed to deliver God's word faithfully and accurately. God has something special and
unique to say about every sphere of life. We could say that
God has a word for business, a word for governments, a
word for families and a word for football. As a great and
mighty King we should expect no less. Our God is no sly,
furtive and insignificant baron who carves out his tiny and
paltry niche (church) and pleadingly begs – can I have this
please? No; our God lays claim to every area of life and
informs us – this belongs to me.

Institutions can be redeemed

Each group of people has been entrusted with a task and
should do this faithfully without bullying and harassing
other institutions and organisations. For example economic life is important. We desperately need bread, butter,
tea, coffee, carpets, shirts, vases, porkpies, screwdrivers

and vacuum cleaners. To lack such goods would plunge us into the most abject poverty and misery. However economic activity must respect God's laws about justice, mercy and Sabbath rest. Economic activity should never become the all-consuming juggernaut it can often become. Business activity is important, indeed crucial, but limited. The beautiful game comes with similar strings attached.

Just the other day I popped round to Jim's house for a cup of tea and I was surprised to find the lad unpacking box after box of tea, coffee, rice and chocolate. 'What on earth are you doing, oh uncouth one?' I yelped. Jim explained to me that he had decided to become a rep for the Traidcraft public limited company. 'Yes, but Jim,' I pleaded earnestly. 'You are supposed to be a football maniac who is besotted with the game and you will ruin the tone of my book if you suddenly abandon the game we love and fling down the gauntlet at the evils of international capitalism. Prithee which hornet has stung your behind?'

Jim waxed lyrical.

'Rocky, you lack knowledge and insight. Listen and learn, oh pompous one. Traidcraft is the UK's largest fair trade organisation and was set up in 1979 to challenge the unfair way in which international trading systems are usually structured. Traidcraft operates on the principle that by paying a fair price for the products we buy, and establishing long term relationships of partnership and co-operation, we can help poor communities to work their way out of poverty and create a much fairer world. Most of Traidcraft's trading partners are community-based enterprises and associations of small holder farmers organised for the benefit of their producers and growers. Traidcraft can give producers access to credit which allows them to buy the raw materials they need.

Traidcraft is a Christian public limited company which welcomes co-operation with all who share a concern for fairer trade.'[13]

Then Jim explained to me that just as we can glimpse signposts of the kingdom of God in the Bristol Church League, so we can see God at work redeeming economic life in the work of Traidcraft. I gasped with surprise and admiration as Tickner berated me for my ignorance about this public limited company and its shalom-filled business vision.

In conclusion we should perhaps add that there is absolutely nothing wrong with using drama, humour or even football in a church service. That is perfectly healthy and acceptable. But we must insist that the kingdom of God embraces far more than just church activities. God is at work invading all of life. At the end of the day it all belongs to the Crucified One who will one day be crowned Lord of lords and King of kings.

[13] See the Traidcraft website at www.traidcraft.co.uk.

9

How do you enter the Kingdom of God?

To say that Bertie Bloggs was gobsmacked would have been an understatement. He had just opened the door and Sir Alex Ferguson was standing on his doorstep grinning and radiating warmth and bonhomie. Bertie had been loafing in his small terraced residence in north Manchester and the house was untidy, dirty and aesthetically impoverished. Bertie had just completed a three day bender with his mates and the empty cans of cheap lager and half-eaten kebabs were lurking in every nook and cranny of the squalid hovel. Unpleasant odours wafted into the nostrils of the Manchester United supremo but the famous knight seemed oblivious to it all.

'I've got some unexpected good news for you Bertie. Can I come in?' Bertie's pulse quickened as he led the VIP into the very bowels of his modest abode. Shaken and bemused, Bertie was unable to communicate succinctly and eloquently.

'Can I get you a cup of Bovril, Mr Ferguson?' blathered the corpulent and dishevelled Bloggs.

'No thank you,' replied the genial supremo, 'but a cup of tea would be very welcome, if you wouldn't mind.' Bertie retreated to the mouse-infested kitchen and plugged in the kettle. Why on earth was Sir Alex sitting in his hideous sitting room? mused the unemployed and penniless scallywag. Just then Bertie became acutely aware of his throbbing, pulsating head and he belched loudly and forcefully. He felt sick and ashamed of his lifestyle, his gluttony, his heavy boozing and his dingy home. Why would a very important and busy man like Ferguson condescend to visit an obese and frankly unattractive loser like Bertie? Something very fishy was going on.

No one is good enough

Jim is a decent enough player. One Saturday I had the opportunity to watch him in action. If I were to compare Jim's prowess as a footballer with my other pals (Tim and Adrian) I would have to conclude that he is the best player that I am personally acquainted with.

Let's turn now for a few moments to consider some of the great players who ply their trade in the premiership. Consider for a moment the silky skills of Dennis Bergkamp. I think we would all agree that the boy Dennis is a consummate ball-merchant. I love his little flicks and his threaded passes. Do you remember that exquisite goal he scored against Argentina in 1998? Recall to mind that several years ago Dennis not only won the goal of the season but all three of the top goals were scored by the Dutch magician. Absolutely incredible. And what about the diminutive Gianfranco Zola? The word *subtle* takes on a new meaning when we patiently attend to the deft ball-skills of this Italian master. Thierry Henry is another player who deserves our close attention. The combination of electrifying pace and gravity-defying close control commands respect. And there are many others we could mention.

These players have been gifted with rare and unusual talent by the Supreme Gaffer and we should be grateful to the King of kings for bestowing his gifts so lavishly and abundantly. As to whether these players thank the Supreme Supremo for these extraordinary gifts only they can say. But there is one sharp conclusion that we can make. Jim is not nearly good enough to play in the premiership! Tickner is not strong and skilful enough to play in that august and exalted company. Paul Scholes is good enough. Robbie Savage makes the grade. Joe Cole gets the nod. The Everton wunderkind Wayne Rooney has more than enough talent to earn his place in England's finest league. However, Jim knows in his heart of hearts that he does not make the grade.

However hard and difficult it may seem to enter the dizzy heights of premiership football, it is at least possible to make the grade. The vast majority of journeymen footballers lack the required fitness, strength and technique. But a tiny minority of players can earn the right to play with Bergkamp, Zola and Henry. We could say that they are entitled to play at that level. They've passed the relevant football A level and they're in.

But entry into the kingdom of God is an entirely different affair! No one is good enough. Mother Teresa isn't good enough. The Archbishop of Canterbury isn't good enough. The Pope isn't good enough. Neither is Sir Cliff Richard. The boy Paul made this point very clear in his letter to the Romans

> There is no-one righteous, not even one; there is no-one who understands, no-one who seeks God. All have

turned away, they have together become worthless; there is no-one who does good, not even one.

Romans 3:10–12

Jesus and murder

My Canadian wife, Anne, has often pointed out to me how much we British enjoy our murder mysteries. Have you ever watched *Morse* or *A Touch of Frost*? I don't know about you but I love that kind of stuff. I find the plots hard to follow and I never guess the murderer correctly but the suspense and the uncertainty of the murder mystery always leaves me gagging for more. Although Jesus had probably never heard of Endeavour Morse or Jack Frost he talked about murder in one of his most famous sermons. He was up a mountain at the time and this is what he said

> You have heard it was said to the people long ago, 'Do not murder, and anyone who murders will be subject to judgment.' But I tell you that anyone who is angry with his brother will be subject to judgment. Again, anyone who says to his brother, 'Raca,' is answerable to the Sanhedrin. But anyone who says, 'You fool!' will be in danger of the fire of hell.

Matthew 5:21,22

Most of my readers, and certainly Jim and I, have never committed murder. Of that there can be no doubt. If Jesus had merely mentioned murder in this great sermon then we could sit back and congratulate ourselves on our smug and easy virtue. We could nonchalantly raise our thumbs and declare unanimously: 'We're all right! We're good enough to get into the Almighty's team of saints and righteous ones. Crack open the beer lads – we've made it into the top team!'

Unfortunately Jesus ups the ante in a quite outrageous and disturbing fashion. He presses home his point by cutting deep into our sin-stained hearts. If we have murderous and angry thoughts about our neighbour then we have broken God's law. This is now becoming painful and the easy elation of raising thumbs in self-congratulation is no longer possible. I don't know about you but I have had murderous thoughts. So too has Jim. Let's face it, if you belong to the human race you will have had such thoughts. This is part and parcel of living in a fallen world.

In this famous sermon Jesus opens our eyes to the depth and the serious nature of our sin and it's difficult to stomach. We have failed miserably to live as God intended. Just look around you and examine the poison of human wrongdoing. It's everywhere and it stains all our seemingly virtuous deeds.

Comical football vignette revisited

It's difficult to overstate just how unpleasant and odious Bertie was. Not only did he stink of stale beer but his teeth were crooked and yellow. His clothes reeked of tobacco and sour goat's cheese. Bad breath and body odour combined to lethal effect as Bertie proffered Hobnob biscuits to his wealthy and famous guest. The great man began to speak.

'Bertie Bloggs, the directors of Manchester United have decided to do something very unusual and unexpected. They have decided to allow a totally unknown player to play in David Beckham's forthcoming testimonial. As you are probably aware Real Madrid will be playing at Old Trafford next month and you have been chosen to play for the team. Not only this, but you will receive 10 per cent of the gate money which could add up to several hundred thousand pounds. What do you say? Would you like to play in David's testimonial?'

Bertie could not move for several minutes. His heart seemed to have stopped and he looked dazed and terror-stricken. Surely this must be a horrible joke. Suddenly the doorbell rang. Bertie slowly regained his composure and went to the door. As he opened the door he was greeted by David Beckham.

'Are you all right?' chirped David. 'Cat got your tongue? Yes, it's all true. You are going to play in my testimonial and you will get at least £200,000 for your efforts. It doesn't matter how badly you play. You've been picked. Get your coat on. You're coming round to me and Victoria's for a slap-up meal.'

Entitlement theology and grace

At the end of the day none of us can march into the Supreme Guvnor's presence and boast about our good deeds. Can you visualise the following encounter with the Almighty?

> Look, Boss. I've worked very hard to bring your king-dom to earth. I helped several old grannies to cross the road and I gave a fiver to that dirty beggar. Don't forget how I helped Aunty Muriel on many occasions to do the washing-up and I lent that widow two hundred quid when she was hard up. Further I refrained from mur-dering that swine Dobson and I certainly did not commit adultery with Tina Thomas. I never stole Julian's pen

and I looked after my gerbils very successfully. I tried hard to be a good husband. Look at me, Gaffer of gaffers – you owe me one. I jolly well am entitled to my inheritance in the kingdom of God. Give me my entry permit now! I've earned it.

It would be a very foolish punter who laid out this kind of entitlement theology when they finally meet the Almighty on the day of judgment. Many of the parables that Jesus told make precisely this point. The people who trust in their own goodness will be disappointed on that final day. Only people who cast themselves on God's mercy will be allowed to enter the kingdom. Here is one of those parables

> To some who were confident of their own righteousness and looked down on everybody else, Jesus told this parable: 'Two men went up to the temple to pray, one a Pharisee and the other a tax collector. The Pharisee stood up and prayed about himself: "God, I thank you that I am not like other men – robbers, evildoers, adulterers – or even like this tax collector. I fast twice a week and give a tenth of all I get." But the tax collector stood at a distance. He would not even look up to heaven, but beat his breast and said, "God, have mercy on me, a sinner."
> I tell you that this man, rather than the other, went home justified before God. For everyone who exalts himself will be humbled, and he who humbles himself will be exalted.'
>
> Luke 18:9–14

It might be helpful to say something about the Pharisees at this juncture. They were a group of Jews who taught and explained their interpretation of the Mosaic Law to the Jewish people. In many respects they had twisted and perverted the original meaning of the law (Mk. 7). Often they were preoccupied with cultic and ceremonial aspects of the Jewish faith – such as the precise amount of spices and herbs that should be tithed. In many respects they neglected the larger themes of justice and mercy that we discussed in chapter 3. Originally the Jewish faith had taught that humans could only enter God's kingdom by trusting in God's mercy. Many Pharisees, however, had rejected this teaching and began to stress that humans could earn entry into the kingdom as a reward. This clearly was an entitlement approach to salvation.

We could say that Jesus recaptured and deepened the original Jewish teaching that humans can never earn God's forgiveness; we can only receive it as a gift of grace. This is how the boy Paul explained this important idea:

> For it is by grace you have been saved, through faith – and this not from yourselves, it is the gift of God – not by works, so that no-one can boast. For we are God's workmanship, created in Christ Jesus to do good works, which God prepared in advance for us to do.
>
> Ephesians 2: 8–10

The word grace is crucial in this passage. God comes to us and offers us friendship and forgiveness as an act of undeserved mercy. We don't deserve God's mercy at all but God comes to us unexpectedly and whispers in our ear: 'You can play for my team! This is my great gift to you.' Paul adds that the person who truly responds to God's great mercy will do good deeds out of gratitude for this gift. It's a bit like when my son Emile kisses me when I have given him his birthday gift. He can't buy that gift; he can't get hold of it. He doesn't have any money, poor blighter, but he can respond to me with gratitude. At the end of the day that's all we have to do with God.

Conclusion of comical football vignette

It was a warm summer's evening when Bertie turned out for Manchester United in David Beckham's testimonial. He glanced around and noticed that Juan Sebastian Veron was furtively picking his nose and Nicky Butt was gobbing enthusiastically. He had been astonished at how kindly the famous players had treated him. Even Roy Keane had grunted a few words of welcome. There had been no sneering references to his flabby body and his lack of physical beauty. Indeed the players had gone out of their way to welcome him. Paul Scholes had told him a couple of great gags and Ryan Giggs had struck up a conversation with him about the precise speed of whippets. Sir Alex Ferguson had spoken warm, soothing words before the game and was most solicitous as to Bertie's emotional well-being. The gaffer really couldn't do enough for the rotund and physically repulsive ex-welder.

The game kicked off at eight o'clock and Giggsie hared up the left wing like an over-enthusiastic cheetah. Raul exuded existential angst and ennui as he chipped the ball down the wing and Ronaldo displayed his toothy grin with relentless frequency. Ruud van Nistelrooy scored a sublime header in the thirteenth minute and not to be outdone Roberto Carlos unleashed one of his more spectacular banana free-kicks which punctured the back of the net. The score was now 1-1 and back heels and showboating became the order of the day. Bertie, alas, was unable to contribute to this extravagant football fiesta.

He was nutmegged on thirteen separate occasions and he even managed to score an own-goal. Bloggs spent most of the game waddling about the park like a bloated whale but nobody seemed to mind. At the end of the game Real Madrid were the victors by five goals to four; Zidane had scored a hat-trick and Rio Ferdinand had muscled in with a brace of belligerent headers. And then the 67,000 punters in the Theatre of Dreams began to chant someone's name. Was it Beckham's? I hear you cry. Was it Keane's? No. The name that was on everyone's lips was BERTIE BLOGGS. Old Trafford reverberated with the name of the porcine ex-welder. Bertie could contain himself no longer and he began to sob uncontrollably; so great was his joy and delight. How on earth could he express his immense gratitude to the Manchester United supremo? Just then Sir Alex Ferguson ran up to him and embraced him with a warm and affectionate bear-hug. 'Don't you hear, Bertie? They love you. Well done, you old rascal!'

In terms of grace and forgiveness we are all just like Bertie. We have broken God's laws and we stand under God's judgment. The New Testament shows us that we cannot enter the kingdom of God by relying on our own virtuous behaviour. That is not possible. It is for this reason that Christ lived and died in our place. He, alone, lived the perfect life and on the cross he bore the sin of the world. When we were struggling to finish the game, sweaty, exhausted and dead in our sins, Christ took our place. On the cross Jesus was punished instead of us. He died so that we can live. He suffered and experienced death so that we can play football in the age to come!

"I was most surprised that He likes to
be called 'The Gaffer of gaffers.'"

10

Football and the Resurrection

Gabby Logan seemed nervous and tense as she waited for the big interview. She was normally at ease and relaxed when she spoke to Gerard Houllier, Arsene Wenger or Sir Alex Ferguson. She knew what to say and she oozed charm and finesse as she probed the top gaffers with poise and precision. She had grown up in a footballing family and she knew the game. But she had never interviewed The Great Greek Boffin before and she anticipated a tense and difficult encounter. She had tried skimming the master's famous bestseller, *The Republic*, but she had been singularly unimpressed by the Greek master's philosophical perspective. 'I've got a lot more time for Aristotle!' murmured the gorgeous television presenter as she fiddled with her ballpoint pen. Just then the manager of the Pagan All Stars 11 emerged from the opposition's dressing room. Gabby picked up her microphone and smiled as the Greatest Philosopher of All Time greeted her. This is how the interview went:

Gabby: Thanks, Sir Plato, for agreeing to this interview. The question that everyone is asking is why have you suddenly abandoned your position as the greatest thinker of all time to manage a team of pagan journeymen playing football against a team of Christians who frankly should have been ripped apart by lions and bears in the amphitheatres of Rome. Isn't this rather absurd?

Plato: Look, Gabby, I've spoken to the press about this on several occasions. It's all right doing a bit of logic and epistemology but at the end of the day I was getting tired of the showbiz lifestyle, wine, women and song that goes with the philosophical profession. You get slagged off by young pups like that cocky upstart Aristotle and to be honest the money wasn't enough to live on. At the end of the day I felt – enough's enough. It's time for a change. Football seemed like a total change and there you have it.

Gabby: Proclus had a great game. Talk us through his first goal.

Plato: You know – what I love about the boy Proclus is that he really loves the game! Spotter's badge for Porphyry to put the lad clear. He got joy down the left and laid it off for the lad Plotinus who give it the little eyebrows. Proclus juggled the ball and hit it full gun with his left peg. Thirty yarder. Over the moon. Chuffed for the lad.

Gabby: Were you surprised when St Augustine dribbled through your defenders and scored that brilliant equaliser?

Plato: Well, I thought the boy was off-side and the referee must have been paid off by those Christians. That's what comes from believing that nonsense about grace and the resurrection of the body. Unbelievable!

Gabby: Were you annoyed when Porphyry was sent off for that two-legged tackle on Dionysius the Areopagite?

Plato: Yeah. The boy didn't touch the Christian lad. He's an amusement arcade and I never saw the tackle anyway. The ref must be blind. The lad was as sick as a parrot about that.

Gabby: You've beaten this Christian team now. Were you surprised at how badly they played?

Plato: Well, to be honest, Gabby, I do think they've gone down hill over the past few hundred years. They used to play a sweet passing game. You know – keep it on the deck and knock it about but truth be told, they play the same kind of game as we do now. We Platonists, if I can call the lads that, we always play the long ball because we like to keep the ball as near to heaven as we can. We like to kick the ball as high into the air as we can, Gabby, because we're trying to get our souls out of this stinking cesspit and get back to our true home in heaven. That's why a lot of our players train on mountains and pillars.

Gabby: Thank you, Sir Plato.

Christianity and Platonism

One of the most tragic stories in the history of the Christian church has been the way in which platonic ideas have suffocated and corrupted biblical ideas. The early Christian community was preoccupied with redeeming life here and now. As we have seen, they sold their possessions and gave to anyone who had need. Many people glimpsed the kingdom of God in this radical group of disciples and many Jews, Egyptians, Greeks and Romans became converted to the Way. Within a few centuries this was all to change. All the leading church fathers were steeped in platonic thinking and practice.[14] The church fathers were the teachers and communicators in the early Christian churches and they

---

[14] We are indebted to Al Wolters for this important insight.

increasingly borrowed and stole the ideas of the Great Greek Boffin. If Plato had been given a pound for every time that a Christian pinched his ideas then Plato's gargantuan fortune would have made Elton John look like a starving orphan!

At first the early Christians stressed the importance of the resurrection and their beliefs affirmed life on this planet. The entire Old Testament story affirmed the goodness of creation and the goodness of the body. When Old Testament writers spoke about their hope in God, they spoke about the resurrection of the body. This is how Job made this point thousands of years ago

> I know that my Redeemer lives,
> and that in the end he will stand upon the earth.
> And after my skin has been destroyed,
> yet in my flesh I will see God;
> I myself will see him
> with my own eyes – I, and not another.
> How my heart yearns within me!
>
> Job 19:25–27

Job makes it very clear that we will see God one day with our eyes and 'in our flesh'. This passage should remind us of the Garden of Eden and how God enjoyed walking with Adam and Eve in the cool of the day. Christian Platonists like Origen and Dionysius the Areopagite were to reject this life-affirming creed. Their message was staunch, bold and uncompromising. The body is evil and life on this planet is a waste of time. 'Get thee into the desert and crucify the flesh' was their witty and helpful advice. Some people were so taken by this spiritual wisdom that they would tie ropes around their bodies and then suspend themselves in uncomfortable positions for days on end! One zealous monk exposed

his naked body to poisonous flies while sleeping in a
damp bog for six months! There were even those who
lived on pillars for many years. The famous Simeon
Stylites lived uninterruptedly for thirty-seven years on a
sixty foot pillar situated thirty miles from Antioch in a
sun-scorched desert. He endured every extreme of
weather, praying and posturing or standing with arms
outstretched in the form of a cross for as long as eight
hours at a time. You would be ill-advised to invite any of
these Christian Platonists to your birthday bash. They
were not exactly a barrel of laughs and they certainly
had no time for football. In actual fact we are pretty sure
that not one of these ancient Christian Platonists ever
attended a football match.

What are *souls*?

To put this issue starkly and boldly we need to investigate what people mean by the word *soul*. Punters who
are influenced by the Great Greek Boffin insist that your
soul is a funny bit of invisible, spiritual stuff that
indwells your body. The soul is like a little perfect football player who lives inside a big, ordinary and imper-
fect football player. The real *you* is not the big fellow but
the little fellow that is hidden inside you. The soul is an
imprisoned spirit living in a dungeon. This was the view
of Plato and his many influential followers – Plotinus,
Porphyry, Proclus and Iamblichus.

Just as greed, violence and the long ball game have
ruined the beautiful game, so Tickner and I would contend that platonic thinking has twisted and perverted
Christianity. We now need to ask the crucial question.
What did Jesus mean when he talked about the *soul*? The
answer is very simple. Just like the writers of the Old

Testament, Jesus understood the soul to refer to one aspect or feature of the way God has made people. This becomes very clear in the following passage:

> One of the teachers of the law came and heard them debating. Noticing that Jesus had given them a good answer, he asked him, 'Of all the commandments, which is the most important?' 'The most important one,' answered Jesus, 'is this: "Hear, O Israel, the Lord our God, the Lord is one. Love the Lord your God with all your heart and with all your soul and with all your mind and with all your strength." The second is this: "Love your neighbour as you love yourself." There is no commandment greater than these.'
>
> Mark 12:28–31

For Jesus the whole person stands before God. We are incredibly complicated creatures who laugh, cry, eat, sleep, dream, imagine, think, scheme and play.[15] And that's just a fraction of what we do. We are creatures who display many different aspects or dimensions. The whole person has been made to respond to God; this involves our soul but it also refers to our body as well. We could say that our soul refers to our inner, hidden life and our body refers to our outer, public life.

Resurrection bodies

Let's now deepen this inquiry by exploring the resurrection of Jesus. On Friday the true king of the world was tortured, flogged and crucified. On Sunday he rose from the dead and appeared to his disciples. Did he turn up as an immortal soul? Certainly not. Jesus was at pains to

---

[15] We are indebted to Calvin Seerveld for this insight.

insist that he was far more than some ghost, spectre or wraith. This is how Luke reports the actual words of the risen Christ

> While they were still talking about this, Jesus himself stood among them and said to them, 'Peace be with you.' They were startled and frightened, thinking they saw a ghost. He said to them, 'Why are you troubled, and why do doubts rise in your minds? Look at my hands and my feet. It is I myself! Touch me and see; a ghost does not have flesh and bones, as you see I have.'
>
> Luke 24:36–39

The risen Christ ate fish with his disciples and he allowed them to touch his body. Jesus had a new kind of body. The boy Paul tells us a great deal about this new body in his letter to the Corinthians. This is what the lad said

> So will it be with the resurrection of the dead. The body that is sown is perishable, it is raised imperishable; it is sown in dishonour, it is raised in glory; it is sown in weakness, it is raised in power.
>
> 1 Corinthians 15:42,43

When we investigate the full range of football injuries that confront the keen player we can begin to grasp Paul's point. Our present bodies are fragile and puny. Consider these footballing vignettes. The Arsenal striker Thierry Henry once went to celebrate in the corner of the pitch after scoring a goal and required treatment after hitting himself in the face with the corner flag! Back in the 1970s Norwegian international defender Svein Grondalen was unable to play in a crunch game because he had collided with a moose while he was out jogging and in 1975 the Manchester United goalkeeper Alex Stepney shouted so aggressively at his team-mates that he broke his jaw! The Yugoslavian player Milan Rapaic was forced to withdraw from several games after inadvertently poking his boarding-pass in his eye at the airport! The famous Arsenal player Charlie George was once injured because he cut off his big toe while mowing the grass and David Seaman broke a bone reaching for his TV remote control. There have also been countless players who have injured themselves while celebrating after FA Cup finals. And Alan Mullery was unable to play several England matches after straining his back while brushing his teeth![16]

We can only come to one conclusion. Our present bodies are subject to serious decay and damage. Paul, however, reminds us that the resurrection body is imperishable and astonishingly powerful. Perfect for football! It may seem rather ridiculous but I often like to point out to Jim that the resurrection body is similar to the body of the cartoon character Superman. As with any analogy you can press the comparison too far and end up with total nonsense. Of course I am not saying that at the resurrection we will have X-ray vision or suddenly become ill when green kryptonite lurks in a hidden box. Balderdash. However, my point is clear and easily apprehended by Tickner. The resurrection body is vastly more real, more dynamic and more powerful than our present bodily kit.

It is clear from the New Testament that the resurrected body of Jesus will serve as a prototype of the bodies we will receive. A prototype is the original model on

---

[16] We are grateful to the Arseweb football website www.arseweb.com/other/bmj.html which has furnished these intriguing stories.

which all subsequent versions will be based. The kind of body that Jesus received at his resurrection will be exactly the same kind of body that disciples of Jesus will receive at the day of resurrection. Jesus spoke about this great event in the book of John. This is what he said

> I tell you the truth, whoever hears my word and believes him who sent me has eternal life and will not be condemned; he has crossed over from death to life. I tell you the truth, a time is coming and has now come when the dead will hear the voice of the Son of God and those who hear will live. For as the Father has life in himself, so he has granted the Son to have life in himself. And he has given him authority to judge because he is the Son of Man. Do not be amazed at this, for a time is coming when all who are in their graves will hear his voice and come out – those who have done good will rise to live, and those who have done evil will rise to be condemned.
>
> John 5:24–29

Theologians refer to this event as the general resurrection and we need to notice how the whole person rises to receive judgment. If Plato were to read these words of Christ he would snort with indignation. At the end of the day resurrection affirms the goodness of creation that we discussed in chapter 1. Resurrection says yes to legs, thighs, chests, feet, heads, arms, noses, mouths and tongues. Resurrection says: 'Football – you're OK!'

The good news behind all this is that Jesus went through the horrible vortex of death and came out the other side into a new world, a world of deathless creation, still physical but transformed.[17] Jesus went down into the grave and came up triumphant over death, evil and the repulsive accuser – Mr Zebub.

---

[17] We are indebted to Tom Wright for this insight.

To what can we compare this supreme triumph? In footballing terms we all understand how a great player like Ronaldo seemed to have failed in the World Cup final of 1998. I remember watching this game with Jim and a few other pals and we were profoundly disappointed with the maestro. He had a very poor game and we were all falling over backwards to have a pop at the Brazilian. Jim was scathing about the lad and we all felt deflated and punctured by his lacklustre performance. 'He thought he was the best player in the world and look at him now,' would have summarised our attitude accurately. And yet four years later the lad waltzed through the World Cup final of 2002, scored two excellent goals and had a blinder. At the end of the game the television cameras were focused exclusively on the cheerful and victorious Ronaldo and the TV pundits kept saying: 'He's back. We thought he was dead and buried but he's back.' The toothy ball-merchant had proved his critics wrong. The resurrection of Jesus is just like that. Jesus seemed to have failed when he died on the cross. His disciples were depressed, deflated and despondent but three days later he came back from the dead and scored the decisive goal against Mr Zebub and his ugly henchmen. In his death and resurrection Jesus has defeated death and entered into a new and deathless world. Those who love and follow him can join him on this amazing journey. We, too, can go through death and come out the other side with new and astonishingly powerful resurrected bodies!

11

Football and the Age to Come

Big Ron, the seraph, was looking forward to the match. He was excited that Jim and Rocky had preferred him to Frank the cherub and he sensed that his big moment had finally arrived. Seraphs had only been mentioned once in the word (Is. 6) and this lack of media attention had disappointed the big fellow. 'After all,' he mused, 'We seraphs have six wings and cherubim only have four.'

Ron looked back on his long career with considerable pride and satisfaction. The Gaffer of gaffers had commanded him to keep tabs on how humans responded to the cultural mandate as recorded in Genesis 1:28. His brief was simple. He had to inform the Supreme Supremo of any innovative playful activity that humans might discover. The Gaffer had told men and women to look after the garden and unfold its glory. The angel Gabriel had patiently explained to Ron that this process could be compared to an acorn that eventually grows into a mighty oak tree. The garden was dripping with fantastic potential and the Gaffer was looking forward to inspecting the rich fruits of human activity. Ron suddenly realised how special and unusual these human creatures were. 'They have been crowned with glory and honour,' was Gabriel's repeated refrain. Ron could only concur.

Ron remembered the first moment of jollification in the Garden of Eden. This transpired in the glory days before the mutiny muffled the wild cackles of total mad tomfoolery. Adam had perfected a brilliant impersonation of an aardvark and Eve's belly laugh had created quite a stir among the angelic hosts. Frank the cherub had laughed like a demented magpie and Ron would never forget Adam's dazzling tour de force.

Is the world evil and corrupt?

For some Christians today this seraphic vignette would appear ridiculous and implausible. Angels have no interest in the comic performances of women and men. Angelic beings exist in a timeless world where cultural innovation does not really register. For these pious brethren humour and buffoonery are intrinsically profane and *worldly* distractions.

This cartoon (by Simon Jenkins) graphically depicts the mindset of the Christian Platonist. This world is totally evil and fit only to be destroyed. As a young Christian I was told by the vicar's wife that culture, literature, paintings, plays, science and sport would all be burned up at the second coming. She counselled me to devote my life to saving souls and to forget about all those *worldly* things that would one day cease to exist. This mindset is still very influential today. We need now to examine our understanding of the way the word *world* is used in the New Testament.

The word *world* is used in a number of different ways in the word. Sometimes it is used very positively, referring to the bobbydazzler creation that we discussed in chapter 1. The classic passage which illustrates this sense of the word is John 3:16. 'For God so loved the world that he gave his one and only Son, that whoever believes in him shall not perish but have eternal life.'

However, the word *world* is often used by New Testament writers in a very negative fashion. Consider the following passages from the Bible

> You adulterous people, don't you know that friendship with the world is hatred towards God? Anyone who chooses to be a friend of the world becomes an enemy of God.
>
> James 4:4

> Do not love the world or anything in the world. If anyone loves the world, the love of the father is not in him. For everything in the world – the cravings of sinful man, the lust of his eyes and the boasting of what he has and does – comes not from the Father but from the world. The world and its desires pass away, but the man who does the will of God lives for ever.
>
> 1 John 2:15–17

My kingdom is not of this world.

John 18:36a

Clearly this negative usage cannot refer to the good creation that the Supreme Supremo crafted with such evident delight. This would be nonsensical. *World* here refers to the sinful, rebellious world that we discussed earlier in the book. The *world* in this sense speaks of corrupt football, perverted business, twisted humour and rotten politics. In short we are referring to the totality of sin-infected creation.[18] Ron the seraph might help us to grasp this point as we continue his story.

Comical football vignette revisited

Rocky and Jim politely informed the impressive and powerful seraph that he would be playing in goal. Big Ron had observed countless goalkeepers weaving their magic in the eons of time and he smiled inwardly as he knew exactly what to do. He had marvelled at the exquisite timing of Gordon Banks as he dealt heroically with Pele's pulsating header. He had savoured the astonishing agility of Lev Yashin and the outrageous eccentricities of Fabien Barthez. Ron suspected that his seraphic speed and strength would impress the smaller angels.

His mind wafted back to the evil age that had shocked him to the very core of his being. To observe Assyrian soldiers flaying enemy soldiers alive was truly terrifying. Even his first taste of the beautiful game was saturated with misery and suffering. Some ancient Celts had sacrificed a young boy to the goddess Andraste and they had decided on a whim to use the decapitated head as a

---

[18] We are indebted to Al Wolters for this important analysis of the word *world*.

football. Here perhaps was the game in its most sinful and corrupt manifestation. This was worldly football in its most evil form. Ron could feel the entire creation groaning and moaning in pain. This was a tough assignment.

Life in this present evil age

One of the great themes of the apostle Paul is the tension between now and the future. One day we will enjoy a magnificent banquet of aged wines and rich food in the age to come. But now we are merely nibbling at the glories of the kingdom. Our lives are like a finger buffet where we gaze lethargically at lonely porkpies and our sleeves are stained with grease and lard as we wearily search for the missing sausage rolls. Pals barge into us and spill our cheap plonk. Babies scream as aunty Muriel rescues the cocktail sausages from the snapping poodles. Wasps irritate us as uncle Bob bores us with his endless yarns about life in the Royal Navy. Valerie, the fifteen year old daughter of aunty Kath, suddenly tells us that she is pregnant; our faces contort with surprise and indignation as we choke on our mini Melton Mowbrays. The dandelion and burdock has gone flat and Emile the whippersnapper has blocked up the lavatory with vast quantities of pink toilet paper. Such is the present age.

The apostle Paul communicated this finger buffet incompleteness and frustration of life in his finely crafted letter to the Romans.

> I consider that our present sufferings are not worth comparing with the glory that will be revealed in us. The creation waits in eager expectation for the sons of

God to be revealed. For the creation was subjected to frustration, not by its own choice, but by the will of the one who subjected it, in hope that the creation itself will be liberated from its bondage to decay and brought into the glorious freedom of the children of God. We know that the whole creation has been groaning as in the pains of childbirth right up to the present time. Not only so, but we, who have the first-fruits of the Spirit, groan inwardly as we wait eagerly for our adoption as sons, the redemption of our bodies.

Romans 8:18–23

We would do well to notice that Paul does not restrict salvation merely to people or immortal souls. In this passage he accosts us with the staggering claim that God will one day liberate the entire creation from its bondage to decay, disease and suffering. Paul is speaking here about the resurrection of the body and the resurrection of the world. But did Jesus ever speak in such terms? Yes he did. In Matthew 5 he declared that the meek would inherit the earth and later on in that gospel he referred clearly to the resurrection of the world when he replied to a question from Peter

Peter answered him, 'We have left everything to follow you! What then will there be for us?' Jesus said to them, 'I tell you the truth, at the renewal of all things, when the Son of Man sits on his glorious throne, you who have followed me will also sit on twelve thrones, judging the twelve tribes of Israel. And everyone who has left houses or brothers or sisters or father or mother or children or fields for my sake will receive a hundred times as much and will inherit eternal life …

Matthew 19:27–29

Renewal of all things

When Jesus spoke about the *renewal of all things* he was referring to the restoration of both heaven and earth. First century Jewish people had absolutely no concept of going to heaven or slipping off to some ethereal theme park in the bright blue sky.[19] As we have repeatedly stressed throughout this book, the Bible tells us about resurrection in all its magnificent glory. The apostle Paul did speak about being caught up into the third heaven (2 Cor. 12:2) and this has encouraged some Christians to dismiss the earth as evil and worthless. In response to this platonic error we must stress that both heaven and earth will one day be liberated from evil, sin and satanic oppression. Heaven cries out for redemption in just the same way that the earth longs for release. As we voyage further with the mighty seraph these issues will become clearer and sharper.

Comical football vignette continued

Ron could remember the battles and struggles that had dogged his career. There had been fierce fighting in heaven and, at times, he had envied the lives of certain privileged humans who seemed to find life so easy and comfortable. Mr Zebub was constantly skirmishing and foraging with his repulsive henchmen. Ron had spent several months in the former Yugoslavia during the 1990s and the evil exploits of Arkan and his brutal Tigers were accompanied by unseen demonic reducers. For every earthly battle there was a corresponding heavenly encounter. To be totally frank, Big Ron was looking forward to the end of this evil age.

[19] We are indebted to Tom Wright for this important insight.

During these violent escapades Ron was grateful to the Supreme Supremo when he allowed the multi-talented and articulate angel to attend football matches in England. Ron had always enjoyed the English game and his mind wafted back to a blistering crunch game between West Ham and Manchester United. The curious seraph had grown very fond of the poetic ramblings of the football pundit Ron Atkinson and to hear that great man waxing lyrical in the gantry filled him with joyful apprehension. The words of the larger than life Atkinson flowed like honey

> Tell you what Clive, Spotter's badge for Joe Cole to put Di Canio clear. The Italian lad give it three lollipops but he wasn't in the wide awake club when he gives it the full gun and the ball crashes into the crowd scene. By 'eck, Di Canio can be an amusement arcade but I've seen The QE2 turn faster than the French stopper who was moving in instalments. Pity the little ginger fellow got the curly finger and Laurent Blanc seems to be playing from amnesia. Oh tell you what Clive – that was a sweet little eyebrows to the second post from the boy Ferdinand.[20]

The nine foot seraph had struggled at first to understand the complex outpourings of the loquacious former gaffer but he had managed to peruse a copy of *Fields of God: Football and the Kingdom of God* and the excellent glossary of technical terms on page 130 had sated his linguistic curiosity. Big Ron was looking forward to briefing the Supreme Supremo on Atkinson's comical and imaginative use of language. The pleasures of angelic scrutiny of

---

[20]   We are grateful to the website Dangerhere www.danger-here.com/ronglish.htm for its excellent introduction to ronglish.

human cultural formation were truly delightful. A verse from the word popped into his seraphic consciousness – 'Even angels long to look into these things' (1 Pet. 1:12).

God's covenant with creation

Foundational to everything we have been saying about the kingdom of God is that the Boss has made a covenant with the earth. He made it. He loves it. He has promised to uphold it – come rain or shine. This crucial crunch concept crops up in the book of Genesis

> And God said, 'This is the sign of the covenant I am making between me and you and every living creature with you, a covenant for all generations to come: I have set my rainbow in the clouds, and it will be the sign of the covenant between me and the earth. Whenever I bring clouds over the earth and the rainbow appears in the clouds, I will remember my covenant between me and you and all living creatures of every kind.'
>
> Genesis 9:12–15a

When I play football with Jim I love thinking about the rainbow and its eternal significance for our lives on the earth. Our God has made a most solemn promise to look after and uphold our home forever. The Boss has spoken to soil, air, clay, mud, gold, silver, plants, animals, birds and humans and declared: 'I make this promise to you.' Even the great moment of judgment that will come on the world at Christ's return will not destroy God's creation or our cultural development of it. The earth and all its fullness will continue into the new age. The new heaven and the new earth will be a continuation, purged and purified by fire, of the creation we now know.

Comical football vignette continued further

Big Ron had been impressed with the Brazilian ball-merchants during the World Cup final in 2002. He revelled in Ronaldinho's deft flicks and savoured Rivaldo's clever dummies. Instant, effortless control was foundational to the Brazilian game and the thoughtful seraph was chuffed when the entire Brazilian team and support staff publicly knelt and expressed their gratitude to the Boss. This was a glimpse of the kingdom of God. The Brazilian players had played beautifully and Big Ron nodded in approval. There was a whiff of glory and Ron noted in his angelic diary that he thought the BBC displayed their usual cold indifference and secular contempt. A verse from the teaching of Jesus exploded in the seraph's brainy bonce – 'But many who are first will be last, and many who are last will be first.'

The kings of the Earth will bring their splendour into the eternal city

In the book of Revelation we get the point full gun. And no messing. The apostle John doesn't mince his words and gives the curly finger to the platonic punter. This is the ultimate reducer on the Greek mindset and you've got to be watching cartoons if you miss the point by now. Spotter's badge to the disciple who penned the fourth gospel and the final book in the Bible

> Then I saw a new heaven and a new earth, for the first
> heaven and the first earth had passed away, and there
> was no longer any sea. I saw the Holy City, the new

Jerusalem, coming down out of heaven from God, prepared as a bride beautifully dressed for her husband. And I heard a loud voice from the throne saying, 'Now the dwelling of God is with men, and he will live with them. They will be his people, and God himself will be with them and be their God. He will wipe away every tear from their eyes. There will be no more death or mourning or crying or pain, for the old order of things has passed away.'

Revelation 21:1–4

We should notice that the creation of this new earth will be different from the divine crafting of our present earth. When God created the earth it was brand new. It had been created from absolutely nothing which is incredibly impressive and reminds me of Michael Owen's stunner against Argentina in 1998. However, according to John, our future is to be spent on a renewed earth – an earth that is a new and dramatically improved version of the one that already exists.[21] This is exactly the same point that we made with respect to the resurrection body of Jesus.

There is also an intriguing verse in Revelation 21:24 which speaks of the kings of the earth bringing their splendour into the New Jerusalem. This theme strongly supports our contention that obedient shaping and moulding of the creation will be present in God's new world. Wherever humans have struggled to make God smile in art, science, politics and sport etc. there will be purified expressions of that activity in the age to come. The new earth will be filled with both divine and human splendour. The final chapter in our story about the seraph will help us to marinade in this nuance.

---

[21] David Lawrence, *Heaven ... It's Not The End Of The Earth*, 43.

Conclusion of comical football vignette

Big Ron had just dived to his left and pulled off a crack-
ing save as Tickner, crestfallen, buried his head in his
hands. His full gun piledriver had barely bothered the
nine footer; Ron winked cockily at the screaming cherubim whose passion for the game was intense. This was his
big moment and he was determined to play a blinder. In
the thirty-third minute Paul of Tarsus nutmegged Brian,
the former blind mute, and Huldah the prophetess
chipped the ball early doors into the left hand channel.
Big Sol chested the ball down and did three or four lol-
lipops as Michael, the archangel, spun away into empty
space, received the ball and threaded it through for little
Zacchaeus, the former tax collector. Spotter's badge for
Zaccy as he controlled the ball with his cultured left peg
and lobbed the ball thirty yards for the girl Eve who was
steaming in at the second post and flicked the ball into the
back of the net. Ron was quite literally over the moon as
he flew around the new earth in a congratulatory lap of
honour. The girl Eve had made mistakes in the past but all
was now forgotten.

By now Ron was strutting around the penalty area
like a pampered peacock and he began to examine the
assembled throng as they roared their approval for this
scorching encounter. He noticed a small toddler playing
with a gigantic crocodile and a laughing polar bear.
There was a young girl sitting in the gantry who was
commentating on the game and simultaneously reading
the best-selling classic *The Lord of the Rings*! And there
was an old man sitting in the lapis lazuli part of the stadium who was admiring a painting by Rembrandt!
Clearly he was enjoying the game and the portrait without any intellectual confusion or discomfort. Seven
miles to his left the seraph noticed the scientist Kepler

investigating the precise movements of the resurrected stars and Isaac Newton was playing a game of golf. Big Ron folded his arms and smiled. This was heaven on earth and the fun was just beginning. Just then Jim Tickner, noticing that the big seraph was watching cartoons, did a David Beckham floater from the half way line. The nine footer was oblivious to the danger as the ball sailed into the top corner. Then he sprinted to Tickner, embraced him and shouted: 'Spotter's badge for Jim!'

12

Football and the Irrelevant Church

The teacher stood at the front of the class and cleared her throat. She had a challenging assignment and she anticipated a tense encounter with Upper 5 class B. She had been dreading this moment for months and her eczema was playing up again. The class had just finished their GCSE exams and the students were in a boisterous and belligerent mood. Tilly Furkin, the class joker, was on fine form and her chameleonic impersonation of Nigella Lawson was going down a storm. Billy Bodson was garnering some hearty chuckles with his loud and vulgar belching.

Miss Simpson began to speak. 'Can we have some quiet, please! Tilly, can we do Nigella later and Billy, would you stop that dreadful noise. Thank you. Mr Smedley, the Headteacher, has asked me to pass on an important announcement to you. You have all just completed your GCSE Religious Education examinations and we have been impressed with your knowledge of croziers, mitres, cassocks, church organs, vestries, steeples and gargoyles. Well done! But many of you lacked insight into fonts, holy water, pilgrimages and saints days. I'm afraid to inform you that you will have to repeat last year's syllabus again and again until you have achieved the required standard. In fact Mr Smedley would like you all to keep taking GCSE Religious Education until the day you die.'

Billy Bodson was the first student to stand up and proffer his insights on the matter in hand. 'Well I must say, Miss Simpson, I find this very disappointing. I have always craved knowledge and insight. I was hoping to learn about a Christian perspective on art and literature. My inner man has longed to know more about Lewis, Tolkien, Hopkins and Milton. To speak my mind boldly I have an unslakable thirsting after wisdom and philosophical insight and I feel very let down by Mr Smedley's pedagogical conclusions. But I bow the knee to his will. I will carry on regardless and bury my head in the required texts.'

Tilly Furkin was the next to speak. 'Billy has spoken for all of us and I commend his decency, his sensitive scholarship and his nobility to all of you. I had longed so deeply to understand the book of Job and the relevance of the Mosaic Law and the Sermon on the Mount to our modern world but I respect you, Miss Simpson, and hold Mr Smedley in high regard. I join with Billy and vouchsafe my everlasting support. Three cheers for Mr Smedley. For he's a jolly good fellow!'

Jim and I know many people who used to serve the Supreme Supremo with enthusiastic wild abandon. For various reasons they grew tired of the faith and stopped attending church. Others still attend church but find the experience painful, irrelevant and tedious. There are many reasons for this sad reality but let's focus on one.

Body of Christ and the local church

When Jesus came to this earth he challenged the nation of Israel to return to its true calling. God wanted the people of Israel to exude love, mercy, peace, justice, righteousness, stewardship, curiosity and *joie de vivre*. In doing this faithfully they would bring the entire world to God. Pagans like Sheba and Nebuchadnezzar would glimpse the kingdom of God in this holy people and this would bring them into the warmth and shalom of God's presence. Tragically the people of Israel failed to live up to this magnificent calling. Instead of turning people on to God, they turned people away from God. And this made the Supreme Supremo very angry. Jesus was very dispirited and distressed by the hostile reception to his preaching and teaching. He warned the nation of Israel that judgment was just around the corner. They had better wake up and repent or else! Some of these Jewish people did repent but many did not. Tragically the Supreme Supremo did bring a terrible judgment upon the nation of Israel when the temple was destroyed by a Roman army in AD 70.

It was almost as if Jesus was saying: 'Forget the temple and all its restrictive jiggery-pokery and follow me. I am the new temple and anyone who comes to me can find forgiveness for their sins and enter the kingdom of God. The covenant is now open to anyone, irrespective of race or creed.' And so Jesus, the true King of the world, was giving birth to a new people, comprising Jews, Greeks, Egyptians, Welsh, Irish, Spanish, Mexicans, Canadians, Burmese, and even English.

The New Testament refers to this new people of God as the body of Christ. Anybody who loves and seeks to serve Jesus Christ becomes a part of this body. The boy Paul discusses this in copious detail in his letters to the Corinthian church. Now we come to the crucial, crunch issue. Very few Christians understand the difference between the local church and the body of Christ. The local, institutional church is indeed an important and vital manifestation of the body of Christ but there should be many others as well. For example Traidcraft is an important non-ecclesiastical manifestation of the body of Christ. Here people are making and selling tea, coffee, rice, pasta, etc. in a way that makes God smile. Traidcraft demonstrates how the kingdom of God is invading the economic sphere of life. Is Traidcraft a church? No. Does it serve God? Yes. Can we think of any other examples?

Let us remember that Jim (37) is the proud if greying captain of the Bristol Sanctuary 11 and his team plays in the Bristol Church League. Are there any signposts of the kingdom of God in this league? Of course there are. Is this league a church? I don't think so. Again we encounter a non-ecclesiastical manifestation of the kingdom of God. We do not have time or space to explore and examine redeemed banks, credit unions, schools and trade unions but exactly the same point is germane to all these institutions. The Supreme Gaffer has a word for business, a word for government, a word for lending money, a word for education and a word for trade unions. Our God is not some sly, furtive and irrelevant baron. He is the true Lord of Heaven and Earth. The Supreme Supremo has a word for every sphere of life.

Church life must be reformed

Ministers, priests, vicars and pastors are failing their congregations because they are not equipping them to serve God in the non-ecclesiastical spheres of life. Too often they suck people into the church sphere of life which is appropriate for only a small minority of their congregation. Too many ministers are doing a Cedric Puddles and this is tragic. Supposing a manager of a powerful and successful club were to become a disciple of Jesus Christ; what should the minister say to this person?

From our perspective the minister should immediately go up to this person and enthuse

> What a fantastic calling you have. I wish I were in your shoes. You have the opportunity to make this club a fantastic oasis of shalom in this sphere of life. For a start you can encourage your players to be lovers of justice, righteousness and *joie de vivre*. Make sure you play the game in a redeemed way. Encourage laughter, fun and spontaneity. Let your lads dwell on the ball and perfect those lollipops, step-overs and cut-diamond passes. Let God's word for play and celebration break out like a raging fever. Encourage them to read improving literature and not to have tunnel-vision about football. Make sure you do not overplay your players and look after them when they get injured. Honour the wisdom of the Sabbath in all you do.

> For heaven's sake, involve all the spouses of the players. Treat them graciously. Do not allow your players to neglect their families but encourage them to get home on time and prepare the evening meal. Encourage your players to be generous with their wages and support poor football players in third world countries. Perhaps you could set up a friendly relationship between your club and a poor club in Liberia. Make sure you treat your cleaners with kindness and respect. Honour their hard work and make them laugh with joy as you tease them affectionately. If it is appropriate encourage your players to study the word and marinade in God's amazing wisdom.

> Finally you should challenge wherever possible the win-at-any cost idolatry. At the end of the day it's only a

game. A beautiful game but there are many other important things in life.

Of course I have barely scratched the surface. There is so much more to say. It leaves me feeling breathless and giddy with excitement. Too often, however, ministers do not even begin to raise these issues! They are often oblivious to these important concerns because they have swallowed a Greek pagan understanding of the gospel which separates life into *church* and *world*. Too often ministers mumble bland platitudes about being nice, honest and sincere. They might suggest to Sir Alex Ferguson that he should join the Parochial Church Council and welcome people at the door. This is nothing short of tragic.

The supreme irony in all this is that a platonic understanding of the gospel inevitably leads to Christians who relate to their work in a stubbornly secular fashion. I remember speaking to a Christian who taught French in a secondary school. I asked this woman why she was teaching her subject. She told me that learning a foreign language is important for tourism and the economy and that people who spoke French could command higher salaries! She further informed me that her work was not particularly *spiritual* and she hoped to leave teaching and work for the *church*.

Clearly her minister had not equipped her with biblical insights. Is this how Christians should approach their subjects? Do we really want our language students to become profiteers and exploiters? Or persuaders? Connoisseurs? Escapists? Revolutionaries? All of these have been suggested as worthy goals for a languages teacher. What would be a proper Christian goal? How about the suggestion that our students should seek to be good neighbours to those of another culture, whether those they meet on holiday, or those who now reside in their neck of the woods.[22] Those who speak foreign languages can love asylum seekers and show them mercy and sensitivity. We have already noted that the Bible urges us to be kind and tender to vulnerable and marginalised people.

We desperately need to rediscover a much broader understanding of vocation. We need ministers who preach the word and communicate the unsearchable mysteries of the grace of God as revealed in Jesus Christ. We need people who pastor and encourage the faithful. We need people who read out passages from the Bible. We need gifted musicians who imaginatively lead the adoration and worship of the Supreme Supremo. These are all crucial functions of the local church. But we also need Christian philosophers, artists, sculptors, novelists, painters, film directors, bricklayers, plumbers, bakers, football players and managers. Mature, imaginative people who have integrated their faith with their work. We desperately need people who are dripping with wisdom and insight about their particular callings.

Church life must be radically reformed. Ministers and those who preach the word must equip people so that they can serve the Gaffer of gaffers in every area of life. Obviously ministers cannot know everything about these callings but they can alert the congregation to these vital concerns. Too much of church education is a bland, platitudinous purée of thin, vague waftings about goodness and niceness. Too often it condemns people to a lifetime of tedious and everlasting GCSE retakes. That is one reason among many why people fall away.

Let us look forward to the day when Arsene Wenger, Sir Alex Ferguson, Terry Venables and Gerard Houllier

---

[22] We are indebted to Arthur Jones and David Smith for these insights about teaching French.

get out of bed on a Sunday and rush expectantly and excitedly to their local churches. As Gabby Logan interviews 'the hairdryer' on a Saturday afternoon Ferguson abandons all the tired and hackneyed clichés and declares

> I've learnt so much about football and the kingdom of God from my local church, Gabby. I may be a top supremo but there is a Gaffer who knows so much more about the game than me. Would you like to hear more about this Guvnor, Gabby?

Glossary of Technical Terms

Amusement arcade	player who overindulges in clever tricks
Back stick	far post
Chuffed	pleased
Crowd scene	packed defence
Curly finger	refers to a gaffer withdrawing a player from a match
Cut-diamond pass	very accurate pass
Drag-back	show the ball to an opponent, pull it back with foot and turn away into space
Early doors	early in the game
Full gun	powerful shot

Gaffer/Boss/ Supremo/Guvnor	the manager
Grafter	a player whose main job is to chase and tackle
Hollywood ball	ambitious and unsuccessful pass
In instalments	moving very slowly and ponderously
Journeyman	moderate player who ekes out a living in the lower divisions
Killer pass	pass which leads to a goal
Little eyebrows	glancing backward header
Lollipop	clever trick where you wave your foot over a stationary ball
Midfield dynamo	ultra-fit player who covers every blade of grass
Nutmeg	cheekily passing the ball through an opponent's legs
Over the moon	extremely happy
Piledriver	ferocious shot
Playing a blinder	playing brilliantly
Playing from amnesia	disparaging comment about an older player who lacks speed and stamina

Playmaker	a technically gifted player who can open up defences
Reducer	a fierce introductory tackle
Second post	far post
Sick as a parrot	extremely upset
Spotter's badge	clever, perceptive pass
Spreader	player who takes ball from grafter and passes with accuracy
Step-over	show the ball to an opponent, step around it with your leading leg and move away with the other leg
Stopper	burly central defender
Striker	player who is expected to score goals
Utility player	poor player who is not good enough to hold down a regular position
Watching cartoons	living in a fantasy world
Wide awake club	alert and sharp

Bibliography

Atkinson, R., *Big Ron: A Different Ball Game* (London: Andre Deutsch, 1999)

Bent, I. (ed.), *Football Confidential* (Northampton: BBC Worldwide Limited, 2000)

Best, G., *Blessed* (London: Ebury Press, 2001)

Bishop, S., *The Earth is the Lord's* (Bristol: Regius, 1990)

DeMol, K., *Sound Stewardship: How Shall Christians Think About Music?* (Sioux Center, Iowa: Dordt College Press, 1999)

Ferguson, A., *Managing My Life* (London: Hodder and Stoughton, 1999)

Frey, B. and W. Ingram (eds.), *At Work and Play* (Jordan Station: Paideia Press, 1986)

Greenslade, P., *A Passion for God's Story* (Carlisle: Paternoster, 2002)

Keane, R., *Roy Keane ... The Autobiography* (London: Penguin, 2002)

Ladd, G.E., *The Presence of the Future* (Grand Rapids: Eerdmans, 1974)

Lawrence, D., *Heaven ... It's Not The End Of The Earth* (London: Scripture Union, 1995)

Marshall, P., *Heaven Is Not My Home* (Nashville: Word Publishing, 1998)

McGinnis, J., *The Miracle of Castel di Sangro* (London: Time Warner Paperbacks, 1999)

Mouw, R., *When the Kings Come Marching In* (Grand Rapids: Eerdmans, 1983)

Parkinson, M., *On Football* (London: Hodder and Stoughton, 2001)

Ridderbos, H., *The Coming of the Kingdom* (Philadelphia: The Presbyterian and Reformed Publishing Company, 1962)

Roques, M., *Curriculum Unmasked: Towards a Christian Understanding of Education* (Eastbourne: Monarch, 1989)

Roques, M., *The Good, The Bad and The Misled: True Stories Reflecting Different Worldviews for Use in Secondary Religious Education* (Crowborough: Monarch, 1994)

Seerveld, C., *On Being Human* (Burlington: Welch Publishing Company, 1988)

Starkey, M., *Restoring the Wonder* (London: SPCK, 1999)

Walsh, B., *Subversive Christianity* (Bristol: Regius Press Limited, 1992)

Weir, S., *What the Book says about Sport* (Oxford: The Bible Reading Fellowship, 2000)

Wolters, A., *Creation Regained* (Grand Rapids: Eerdmans, 1985)

Wright, N.T., *Jesus and the Victory of God* (London: SPCK, 1996)